AIRCRAFT WEAPONS
OF WORLD WAR ONE

CONTENTS

INTRODUCTION	P.2
DETAIL STUDY OF MAJOR MACHINE GUNS	P.6
GUNNERY TRAINING	P.30
FORWARD FIRING MACHINE GUNS (ALLIED)	P.40
FORWARD FIRING MACHINE GUNS (CENTRAL POWERS)	P.62
OBSERVER'S GUNS (ALLIED)	P.78
OBSERVER'S GUNS (CENTRAL POWERS)	P.106
BOMBS & GRENADES	P.126
CANNONS & RECOILLESS GUNS	P.148

AIRCRAFT WEAPONS OF WORLD WAR ONE
©Canfora Publishing 2023
ISBN 978-91-988425-0-0
Design: Toni Canfora
Print: Printall, Estonia

Canfora Publishing
Industivägen 19
171 48 Solna, Stockholm, Sweden
info@canfora.se
www.canfora.se

INTRODUCTION

IN THE BEGINNING

World War One forever changed the way wars would be fought. In 1914, man had only recently taken to the skies in fragile aircraft. Many of those early "kites" were often as dangerous to their pilots as they were to any prospective opponent. Even so, it didn't take long for the gentlemanly waves and salutes between unarmed pilots to give way to dropping rocks and bricks, dangling grappling hooks, and then progressing to pistol shots and shotgun blasts. No sooner had one man taken flight but he became committed to shooting other men out of the sky. The stage was set for an aerial arms race.

After the Wright Brothers successful flight, interest in aeronautics grew rapidly in the United States. Various flying clubs staged events to advance flying beyond the level of a hobby, and to attract the interest of the American military. In August 1910, 300 feet above the Sheepshead Bay racetrack on Long Island, New York, US Army Second Lieutenant Jacob Fickel clutched a wing strut of an early pusher aircraft (piloted by aviation pioneer Glenn Curtiss) and fired four shots from a Springfield M1903 bolt-action rifle at a target below. The first recorded firing of a firearm from an aircraft yielded surprisingly good results: two of Fickel's shots were in the bullseye.

In August 1912, America witnessed another first in military aviation. US Army Lieutenant Colonel Isaac N. Lewis had recently created a new machine gun for the Automatic Arms Company of Buffalo, New York. Colonel Lewis' gun was a modern design, much lighter than most of the era, and fed by a detachable drum magazine. Lewis

An early Lewis gun, the first machine gun fired from an airplane, June 7, 1912

The Luger P08 "Lange Pistole" as used by the pilot.

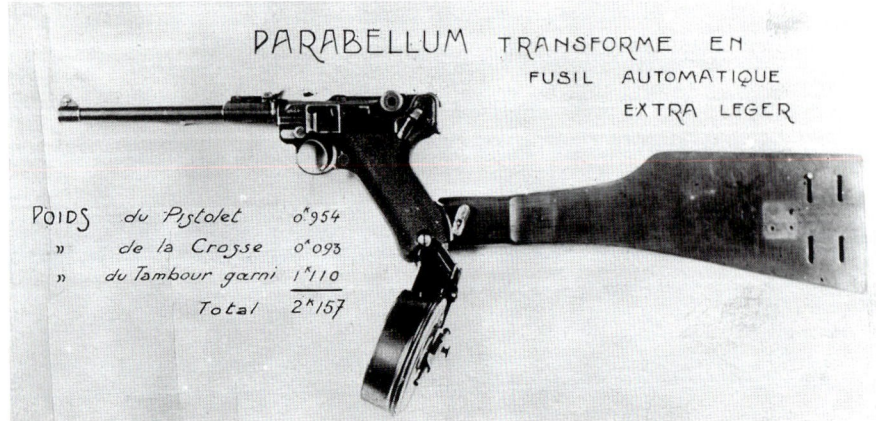
Pistols like the Luger P08 (Lange Pistole 08) with its 7.9-inch "artillery barrel", 32-round drum magazine, and shoulder stock were in the mix of early semi-automatic weapons to provide flexible aerial firepower. Unfortunately, pistol rounds like the 9mm Parabellum did not have the range or power to be of much use.

A pistol for the Royal Flying Corps: The Webley Mk. VI (.455 Webley) top-break revolver.

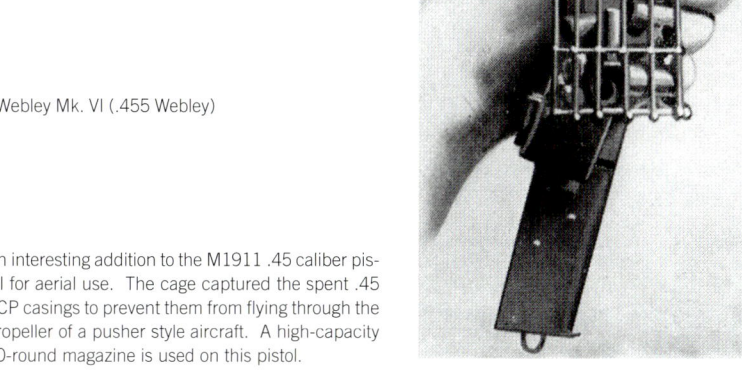

An interesting addition to the M1911 .45 caliber pistol for aerial use. The cage captured the spent .45 ACP casings to prevent them from flying through the propeller of a pusher style aircraft. A high-capacity 20-round magazine is used on this pistol.

The US M1903 Springfield Air Service Rifle: A modified M1903 rifle (.30-06) with a shortened stock and handguard, a simplified rear sight, and a 25-round extension magazine. (Courtesy of Bruce Canfield)

was a dynamic thinker, and shortly after he produced the first few examples of his now famous gun, he envisioned using the 25-pound weapon from an aircraft.

At the US Army's Pilot Training School at College Park, Maryland, Lewis' plan came to fruition. The school Commandant, Captain DeForest Chandler, offered to demonstrate the airborne firing of the Lewis gun personally. After a short training class from Lewis on how to handle the weapon, Captain Chandler boarded a Type B Wright pusher aircraft, with Lieutenant T. DeWitt Milling serving as pilot. The Lewis gun was strapped between his legs, with the muzzle resting on the top of the aircraft's foot-rest crossbar. A 6x7' target made of cheesecloth was placed on some open ground near the rear of a hangar. Three passes were made from about 250 feet, with Captain Chandler firing a short burst each time. Even though Chandler had no sights and could not see the impact of his rounds, it was discovered that he hit the target five times, with several strikes very close by. The next day they tried it again (with Lt Roy Kirkland piloting) and were rewarded with even better results: 14 hits out of 44 shots fired. Suddenly, the aircraft and the machine gun were forever joined.

Newspapers around the USA reported on the event and thousands of people saw the now famous photo of Captain Chandler with the Lewis gun aboard an aircraft. Many additional stories were written about the airplane's potential as a military weapon. Even so, the US Army was not interested in arming their aircraft with anything. The General Staff made it quite clear that aircraft were

The Mondragon M1908 Rifle: The semi-automatic Mondragon rifle (7x57mm Mexican Mauser) was made in small numbers by SIG in Switzerland and was adopted by the Imperial German Flying Corps as the Fl.-S.-K. 15 (Flieger-Selbstladekarabiner, Modell 1915). The Germans ultimately developed a 30-round drum to replace the Mondragon's original 10-round box magazine.

good for scouting, and nothing else. The nation that created the airplane, and gave birth to the Lewis Gun, refused to combine the two to take the lead in military aviation, even as the world edged closer to war.

UP FROM THE MUD

While much of the Great War ground combat became mired in bloody stalemate, the combatant air forces sought to get infantry machine guns out of the trenches and into the skies. It was not as easy as anyone suspected. Machine guns themselves were relatively new, and supplies remained limited while war industries on both sides struggled to produce them in quantity. Meanwhile, the concept of a "light" machine gun was essentially unheard of. At a time when the tiny, fragile aircraft of the era needed compact firepower, most machine guns weighed in at more than 40 pounds, even without ammunition.

Except for the French Hotchkiss M1914, the primary machine guns of WWI were water-cooled, designed with hefty water jackets to allow for extended firing without overheating their barrels. Air crews were far less concerned about overheated barrels, as the ambient temperatures at altitude were often coolant enough, with the continuous airflow also a cooling factor. But machine guns had not been designed with the needs of airmen in mind, and so the modifying processes began—converting water-cooled guns to air-cooled and finding ways to mount the cumbersome weapons in the rear cockpit for the observers to use without shooting off parts of their own aircraft.

Early on, the Lewis gun established itself as the most versatile aircraft MG of the Great War. The Lewis quickly evolved from its original infantry gun configuration, losing weight by shedding its wide cooling jacket, replacing its shoulder stock with a spade grip, and expanding its ammunition drum

The first successful machine gun mounts were on "pusher" style aircraft, as depicted on this Voisin III, in a wartime painting by France's Henri Farre.

In April 1915, the arrival of the Fokker Eindekker and its synchronized gun, brought on the six-month "Fokker Scourge", and forever changed the nature of aerial warfare.

capacity from 47 to 97 rounds. The Lewis was primary weapon for Allied observers and defensive gunners. While it was never a synchronized forward gun, the Lewis was also mounted in several top-wing configurations to fire above the propeller arc. Despite its advantages, the Lewis gun wasn't perfect—it was difficult to load the ammunition drums in flight, and the later twin-gun Scarff mounts required considerable strength for the gunner to maneuver.

ABOUT THIS BOOK

This volume was a long time in the making, and the timeline to collect the photographs was painfully slow. Even so, Toni Canfora and I were very excited about the opportunity to document the aerial weapons of World War One. I am grateful for his dedication and craftsmanship to produce this photo study. Working with century-old images takes particular care and Toni has the design skills to make look great in the 21st Century. The aviators of the Great War were incredibly brave, and their combat experience was a very personal one. So too was their relationship with their aircraft and its weapons. From the earliest airborne firearms and air-dropped ordnance of 1914 to the heavily armed airplanes of 1918, we've done our best to give you a comprehensive view of the aerial weapons of World War One. This collection of photos is our tribute to the first warriors of the skies.

Unless otherwise noted, the images contained within this book come from the United States National Archives, the Library of Congress, the USMC Historical Division, the United States Air Force, and the author's collection.

We would also like to express our gratitude to Viktor Kulikov for providing photos and information from his archive.

Early forward-firing guns came in several configurations - including an angled that fired just outside the propeller arc. Reloading the Lewis drum magazine in flight was an awkward proposition.

Early Lewis aircraft guns were modified infantry guns with their cooling sleeves and buttstocks removed (or cut down). This Lewis carries a 97-round drum.

DETAIL STUDY OF MAJOR MACHINE GUNS

Learning to fly and fight: A US Army Air Service cadet training with a US Model 1917 Lewis gun, converted for air use with the removal of the buttstock and addition of the spade grip. Ring and bead sights are clamped to the radiator cover, and an infantry type 47-round drum magazine is used.

LEWIS

The Lewis gun is a particularly vital element in the story of WWI aircraft machine guns. Designed in America, but not initially accepted there in appreciable numbers, the Lewis was briefly produced in Liege, Belgium before manufacturing was moved to BSA at Birmingham, England shortly before the war began. Demand for the Lewis as a light machine gun for British ground troops was immediate. As Allied aircraft became armed, the Lewis was found to be readily adaptable for aerial use, its shoulder stock quickly replaced with a spade grip. Further modifications soon followed, stripping away the radiator and its casing, and saving weight any way possible. By 1916, the Lewis' distinctive drum magazine (originally containing 47 rounds) was increased to 97 rounds. Several attempts were made to synchronize the Lewis, but these were never successful enough to use the MG as a synchronized forward gun. Even so, the Lewis was used by all Allied air forces, and the Germans also used many captured Lewis guns. Until late in 1918, there were never Lewis guns to meet the demand. Lewis guns were manufactured at BSA in England, Savage Arms in the USA, and small amounts by Darne in France.

The standard Lewis Gun: Designed in America, first produced in quantity in England, and nicknamed "The Belgian Rattlesnake". At 28 pounds, the Lewis was the preeminent light machine gun of World War One.

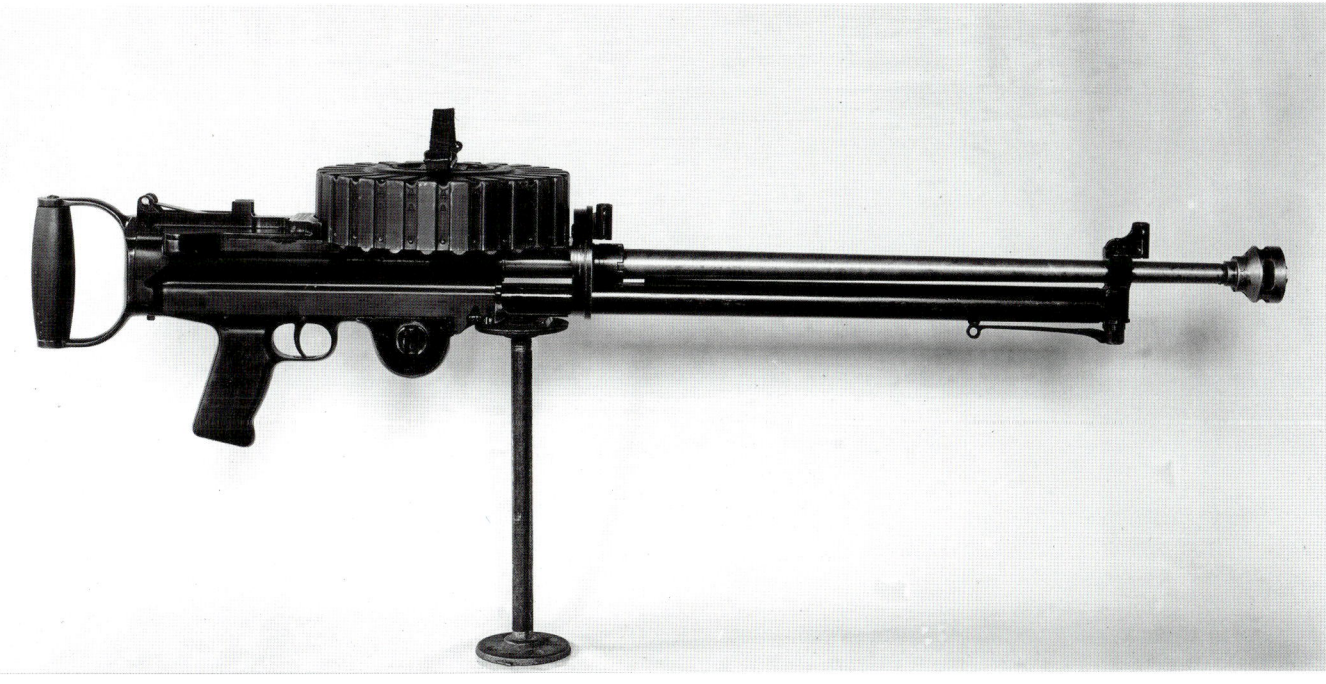

The M1918 Lewis aircraft gun. This example, chambered in .30-06, was made in the USA by Savage Arms. Note the American "recoil check" installed on the muzzle.

DETAIL STUDY

The Model 1917 showing its shell deflector bag to catch spent casings.

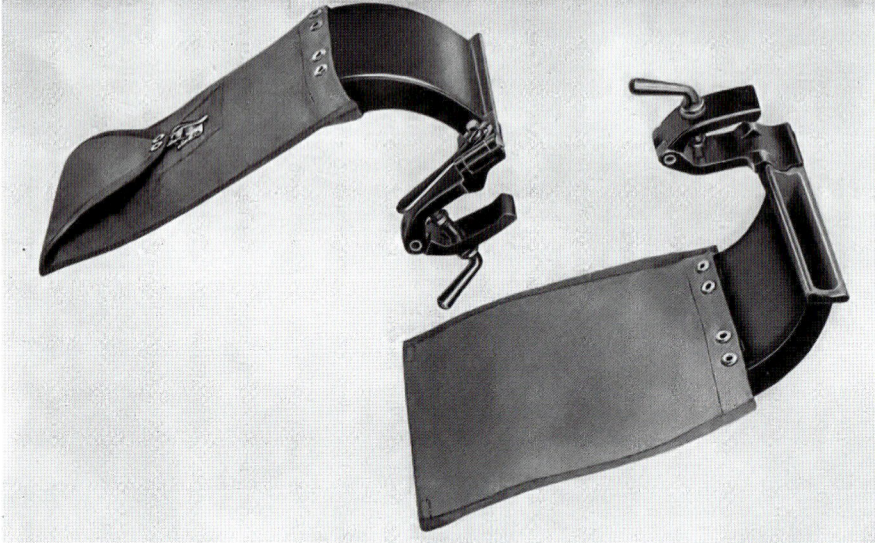

The "deflector bag" for the Lewis aircraft MG, designed to capture ejected shell casings.

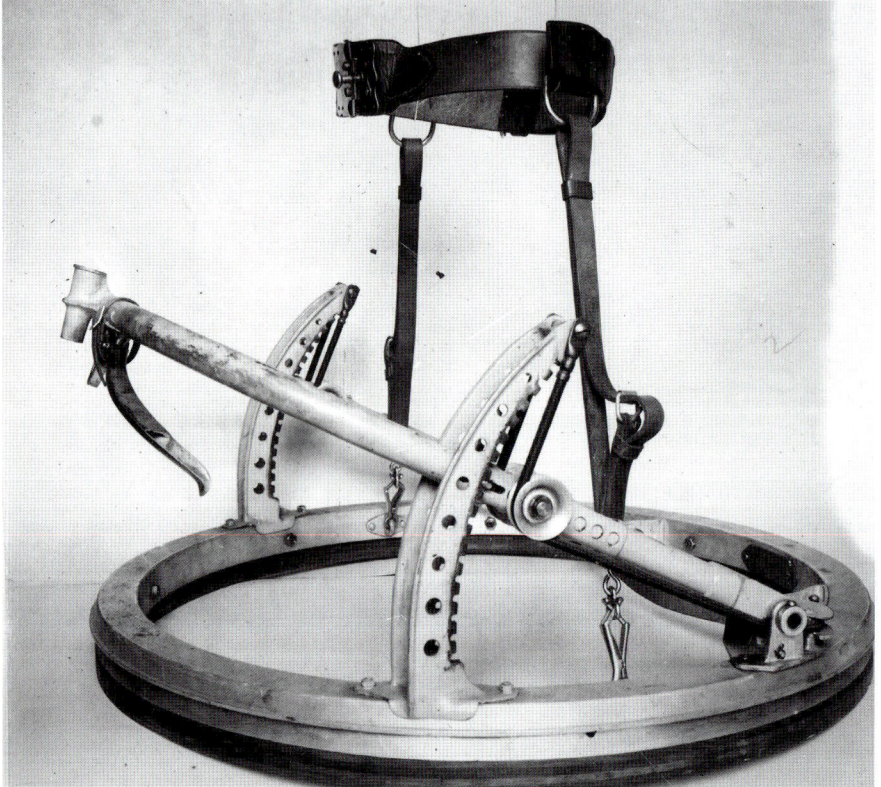

The French TO-3 "tourelle" mount could accommodate one or two Lewis guns. Note the leather safety harness for the gunner.

The Lewis' 97-round drum magazine developed for aircraft use.

Studio view of a Scarff ring equipped with folding shoulder stocks.

The search for greater firepower: An experimental triple Lewis gun configuration made by the Frederick Pearce Company in New York City during late 1918.

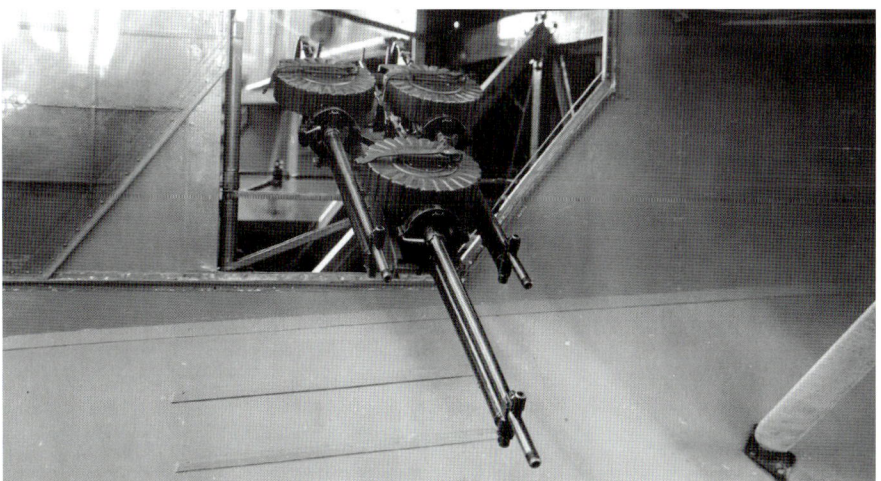

A triple Lewis gun mount in the beam position of a US Navy Curtiss F-5-L flying boat.

A US Model 1918 Lewis (with a Norman van front sight) on Foster mount. Note the Aldis sight ahead of the windscreen.

A "RNAS pattern" Lewis with a 47-round drum magazine. Note the remote trigger control cable.

This photo of a Nieuport 17 cockpit demonstrates that the top-wing Lewis could be fired upwards at an angle into the unprotected belly of an enemy aircraft. This is a "stripped" Mk.I Lewis on a twin pylon mount.

A British MkII Lewis made for the Royal Flying Corps. This gun is fixed to the top wing of a Nieuport 27 Foster mount (No. 5 Mk 1).

Reloading Lewis drums in flight was a difficult procedure. Here a trainee demonstrates the proper technique using the stout leather handle of the 97-round drum.

A French-style twin pylon arrangement for the Lewis gun on the top wing. Note the Aldis optical sight (32-inches long), with a large rubber eyepiece at the rear, and a front cover flap that could be raised or lowered by the pilot.

A Mk.II Lewis swung forward by an R.E.8 observer to fire upwards. Note the large collector bag (also called the Mk.II). The Mk.II Lewis featured a thin metal tube to protect the barrel and gas cylinder.

A Lewis on a Scarff mount aboard a Breguet 14 of the US 96th Aero Squadron.

A good view of a US M1918 aircraft Lewis on a Scarff mount — note the later style ring-and-bead sight and the collector bag (officially called a "deflector bag").

A view of the observer's position with twin Lewis guns on a Scarff mount aboard a US-built DH.4.

Ground attack 1918: Twin Lewis guns angled forward and downward for strafing aboard a US DH.4. Most of these strafing modifications were created in the field.

Lewis guns were valuable: A US soldier poses with a pair of French (Darne-built) Lewis guns salvaged from a wreck.

Airmen had to become weapons experts. A deeper understanding of machine guns drove advances in air combat during WWI. Here, British troops clean and repair a Lewis Mk I in a field maintenance shop.

An embarrassment of riches: Racks of US Model 1918 Lewis Aircraft MGs (.30-06) inside the armorer's shed of an American squadron in France.

An American armorer's room in France during late 1918: Lewis, Vickers, and Marlin MGs can be seen, along with a captured German LMG08/15 at the far left of the table.

VICKERS

Simply put, the Vickers-Maxim is a classic machine gun, one of the best ever produced. Introduced into British Army service in 1912, the Vickers MG (chambered in .303 British) would serve on until officially withdrawn in 1967. Originally invented by Hiram Maxim, an American, the Vickers-Maxim collaboration dates to the initial model of 1891. Reliability, stability, and accuracy were hallmarks of the Vickers as an infantry gun, and once the challenge of firing through the propeller arc was overcome, the Vickers carried these same good qualities into the air. The Vickers was used by the British, French, Belgian and American air services in great numbers, and by the Russians and Italians as much as they could acquire. The Vickers was also made in the USA, first came the US Model 1915 (chambered in .30-06) which served with US troops in Europe, and then came the "US Vickers Aircraft Machine Gun, Caliber .30, Model 1918", which equipped many aircraft in the US and French air services in 1918.

A detail view of a US Army Air Service Salmson 2 A.2 nose. The Vickers is a Colt-made gun that retains its blast deflector.

A Colt-made Vickers Aircraft Machine Gun Model 1918, chambered in US .30-06. The device on top of the breech is part of the Birkigt synchronization gear used with Hispano-Suiza engines.

Foolproof reliability: The Vickers MG was praised for its performance for generations. Adopted in 1912, it served in British infantry units until 1968. The gun weighed 40 pounds with a full water jacket. The tripod weighed up to 50 pounds, and a 250-round ammunition belt weighed 22 pounds.

A detail view of the major parts of the Vickers MG.

The 5-inch ring and bead sight normally used with the Vickers aircraft MG are seen at the upper middle and right in this image.

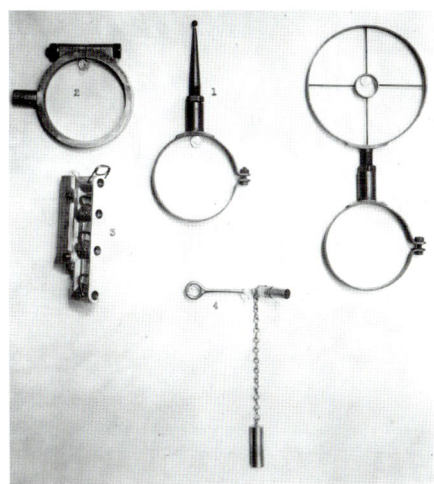

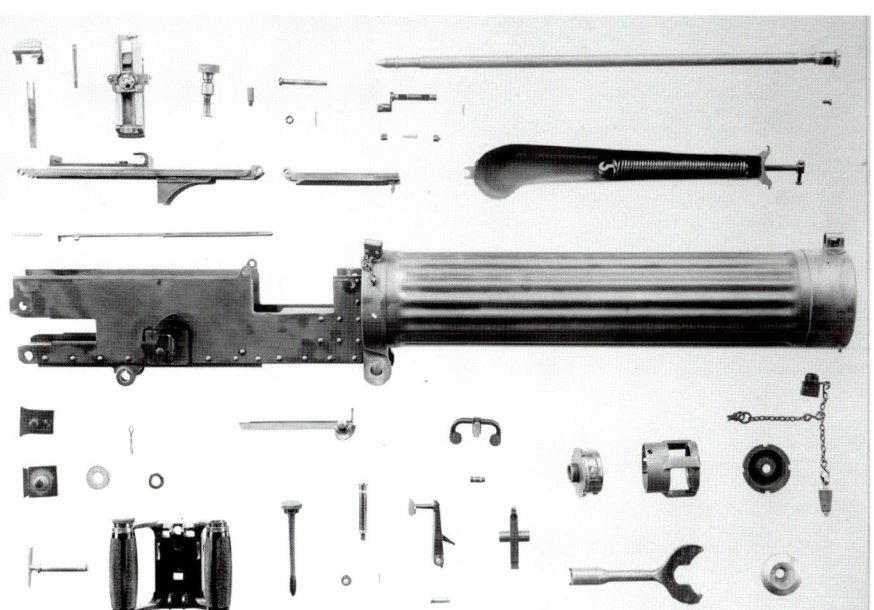

DETAIL STUDY

Synchronizing gear: There were several Allied synchronizing designs. Here are three views of the Birkigt gear. The designer of the Hispano-Suiza engine, Marc Birkigt, also developed a gun synchronization system to go along with it ("Type II moteurs fixes", or informally "Spad Gear"). This system entered service in the autumn of 1916 on the Spad VII C1.

Twin Vickers MGs mounted above the Hispano-Suiza motor of a Spad XIII. Note the blast deflectors below the muzzles of each gun.

The "Balloon Gun": Colt altered about 1,000 Vickers MGs from their Russian contract and rechambered them from Russian 7.62x54R to fire 11mm French ammunition to create the "Gras Vickers"— which offered a useful tracer/incendiary round for anti-balloon work (Desvignes Mark XI incendiary). These guns were indistinguishable externally from a standard Vickers and were used by French and American squadrons.

DETAIL STUDY: MARLIN

During 1915 the Marlin-Rockwell Corporation purchased the production equipment and the manufacturing rights to the Colt-Browning M1895. Soon after, weapons designer Carl Swebilius redesigned the old M1895, replacing the potato-digger swinging arm lever system with a straight-line, gas-actuated piston. The result was the Marlin M1917 and M1918 aircraft guns—faster firing (at 650 rpm) and about eight pounds lighter than the Vickers. Synchronizing gear and ammunition feed channels were late in development, delaying the Marlin's appearance in combat until the autumn of 1918. Most appear to have been mounted to fire forward on US Army Air Service DH.4 and Salmson bombers. Reports on the gun's performance were highly favorable, with pilots remarking that the Marlin was reliable and less inclined to freeze at higher altitudes.

Learning the basics of the Marlin aircraft gun at Princeton University during 1918.

The Marlin 1917 machine gun set up with a trigger motor for the CC synchronizing gear. This gun is set up on synchronization tester at the US Army Air Service School of Aerial Gunnery in California.

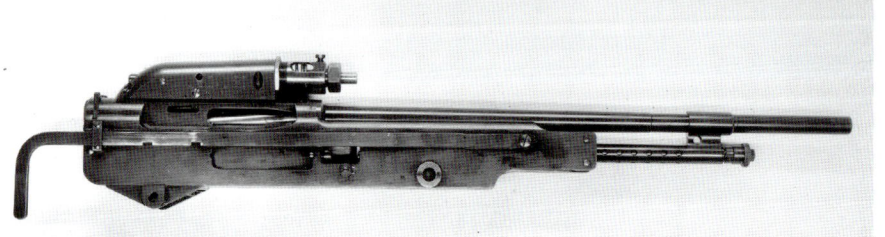

The improved Marlin 1918 aircraft machine gun. Small numbers of these guns arrived in France during the autumn of 1918.

Twin Marlin 1917 guns mounted on a US-built DH.4. This aircraft has a Aldis magnifying gun sight.

The pilot's view: Marlin guns set up for a synchronization test aboard a DH.4. Note the charging handle and the ammunition feed chute to the right.

Synchronization testing on a Marlin 1918 aircraft gun. Note the bullet perforations on the thin wooden disk mounted to simulate the spinning propeller.

SPANDAU & PARABELLUM

Of all the major powers, Germany was best equipped with machine guns at the beginning of World War One. The MG 08 (chambered in 8x57mm), based in the seminal Maxim design, went into full scale production at Spandau in 1908. After the war began, the effort to create a lighter version of the MG 08 for more mobile infantry firepower resulted in the MG 08/15. The 08/15 featured a bipod, pistol grip, and buttstock similar to a light machine gun, but weighing 40 pounds it was anything but "light". Tripod-mounted MG 08s and the marginally lighter MG 08/15 comprised the great majority of German infantry MGs of the Great War.

In the air, once Anthony Fokker created his synchronizing gear, the Germans quickly created the LMG 08, an early conversion of the MG 08 into an air-cooled gun. Soon after came the LMG 08/15, lighter and faster-firing at 600 rpm. Both weapons were highly reliable as Germany's standard fixed forward-firing guns.

For the most part, German observers and defense gunners used the Parabellum machine gun. The Parabellum M1913 began as a water-cooled ground gun, but soon found its place as an air-cooled aircraft gun. The Parabellum M1913's cooling jacket had a distinctive slotted design, and the later M1913/17 had a modern-style, tight fitting barrel jacket. The Parabellum guns were fed by 250-round cloth ammunition belts and cycled at about 700 rpm. Many German observers used a large tubular optical sight on the Parabellum, and the weapon was considered reliable and accurate.

The guns of the Red Baron: British troops examine the LMG 08/15 machine guns taken from the wreck of Rittmeister Manfred von Richthofen's DR.I triplane.

The MG 08 infantry machine gun on the massive "Schlittenlafette" tripod-sled mount. The MG 08 weighed 152 pounds total with the gun, a full water jacket, and the tripod. Its cyclic rate was 500 rounds per minute.

Detail view of the LMG 08/15 aircraft gun. Note the small ring sight at the front of the cooling jacket and the shaft for the synchronization gear.

Overhead cutaway view of the LMG 08/15. This gun has a 08/15 S recoil booster on the muzzle.

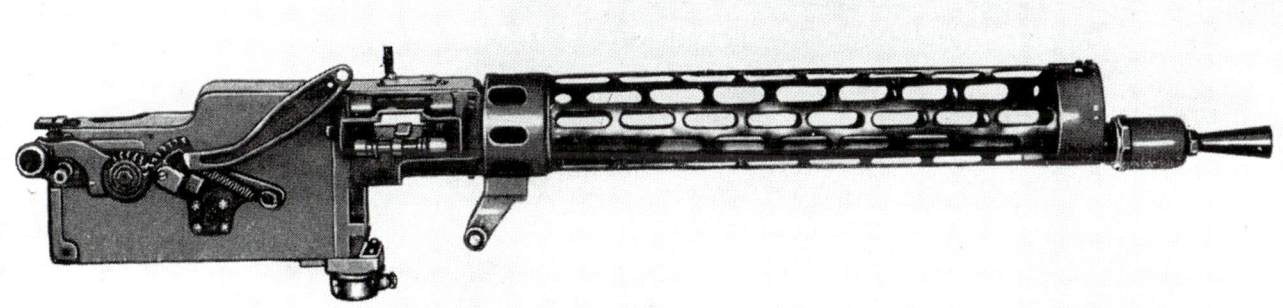

The LMG 08/15 (Luft-MG 08/15) aircraft machine gun which was often called the "Spandau" by the Allies. This gun entered production during May 1916, and approximately 24,000 were made by the end of the war.

The original LMG 08 (Luft-MG08). Developed in 1914, production of LMG 08 dwindled after the introduction of the LMG08/15 in mid-1916. When synchronized the LMG 08's cyclic rate fell to as low as 300 rpm. This damaged and captured example is seen in a NYC art gallery during late 1918.

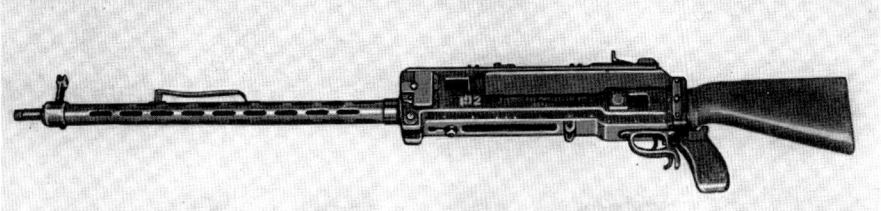

The Parabellum M1913/17 dispensed with the structure of the perforated water jacket and adopted a true form-fitting barrel jacket for an air-cooled MG.

A French pilot poses with trophies from an aerial victory — a pair of Parabellum M1913 guns.

A Parabellum Model 1913 equipped with a 200-round belt drum. A supporting rod connects the drum with the muzzle, helping to maintain the critical 90-degree angle between the ammo belt and the gun's feed mechanism.

Parabellum Model 1913 (7.92x57mm) was the most widely used "free" or "flexible" MG on German WWI aircraft.

COLT-BROWNING M1895

The M1895 was America's first machine gun, originally chambered in 6mm Lee-Navy, and seeing service in small numbers with the USMC during the Spanish-American War. The M1895 was an early air-cooled design, leveraging a heavy barrel. Colt made the M1895 in several calibers, and the gun was relatively popular on the international market. In WWI, Canadian, Italian, and Belgian infantry units used the M1895, and the French and Imperial Russian air services used the weapon on aircraft. The Russians, hard-pressed for machine guns, used the "Colt" (in 7.62x54mmR) in multiple positions, including synchronized to fire through the propeller arc. The old "potato-digger" was a marginal ground gun, badly prone to overheating, but in the chilly skies over Russia, it found new purpose and served on through 1917.

The Colt-Browning M1895. During World War One, the M1895 was used in combat by Canadian, Belgian, Russian, and Italian troops, and used by the French and Russian air services.

The "potato-digger" in use during training at Camp Lewis during early 1918. The nickname comes from the 10-inch-long gas-actuated lever visible beneath the barrel. The M1895's cyclic rate was low, only reaching about 480 rpm.

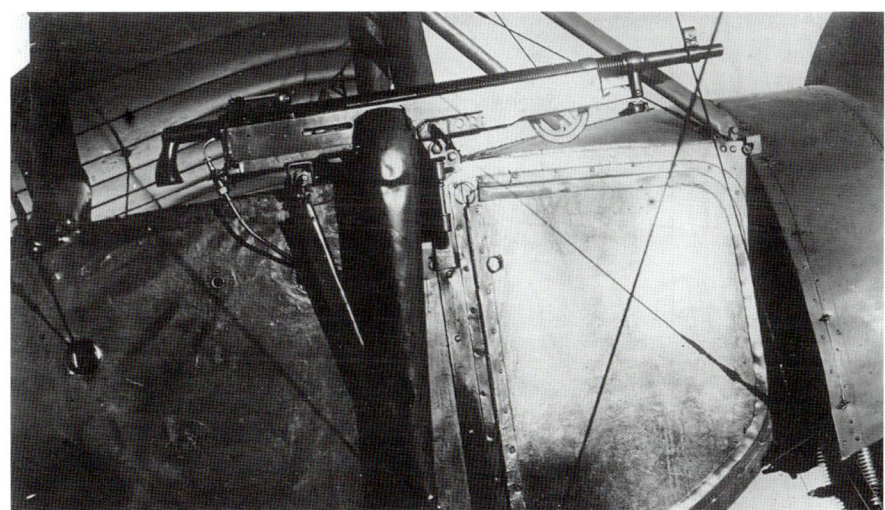

The Imperial Russian Air Service badly needed machine guns, and although the M1895 was a poor choice for this application, it became the most common aircraft MG in Russian service. M1895 MGs (in 7.62x54mmR) were used in a variety of roles, from observers' guns to synchronized mounts, like this example on a Russian Morane. (Via Kulikov)

SCHWARZLOSE

The Maschinengewehr Schwarzlose M.7 (8x50mmR Mannlicher) was the primary machine gun of Austro-Hungarian forces in WWI. It was simple, robust, and reliable as a ground weapon. In the air however, the Schwarzlose proved problematic as a synchronized forward-firing gun—its slow cyclic rate necessitated an engine rpm restriction, and a "Kravics indicator" was regularly fitted to warn the pilot of synchronizing gear failure. The Schwarzlose was commonly mounted to fire above the propeller arc, encased in a Type II VK gun pod. As an observer's gun, the Schwarzlose was first modified by cutting slots into the water jacket, and by 1916 the jacket was removed, and aircraft gun designated the MG-16. The cyclic rate of the MG-16 was improved to nearly 900 rounds per minute.

The Austrian Schwarzlose M.7/12. The gun and tripod combined weighed a little more than 91 pounds. The M.7/12 is fed with a 250-round cloth belt and fires at 580 rpm. (Via SA-Kuva)

A Brandenburg C.1(Ph) 329.50 equipped with a Schwarzlose MG-16 aircraft machine gun for the observer. The MG-16A removed the normal cooling jacket and featured a higher cyclic rate (800 rpm)—feeding from a 250-round spool. A Schwarzlose M7/12 infantry gun is mounted on the top wing to fire above the propeller arc. Note the tall channel that feeds the ammunition belt stored in the fuselage.

The M.7/12 used as a anti-aircraft gun. Note the distinctive wide handles with a central "thumb-trigger".

HOTCHKISS M1909, FIAT-REVELLI & MADSEN

The Fiat-Revelli Modello 1914 (6.5x52mm Carcano) was Italy's standard machine gun of World War I. Although similar to many water-cooled MG designs in the Maxim style, the Fiat-Revelli was not a belt-fed gun. Instead, it used a bizarre "strip-feed box" system with a fragile 50 or 100-round magazine divided into ten or twenty round compartments. Although not a great, or even good, aircraft gun, the Model 1914 was what the Italians had—so they removed the water jacket and provided a new barrel surrounded by a series of heat-dissipating grooves. A bulky collection box was added to catch the spent casings that were ejected out of the top of the breech case. The Model 1914 was not synchronized but was used in top-wing and observer's gun positions until the end of the war.

The Hotchkiss light machine gun was known by several names: The Hotchkiss Mark I, the Hotchkiss Portative, and the M1909 Benet-Mercie. Chambered in French 8mm Lebel, British .303, and US .30-06, the Hotchkiss was an early choice as an aircraft gun, particularly in France. Normally fed by metal 30-round feed strips, a 200-round belt spool was developed to give the gun an extended fire capability. The cyclic rate was about 600 rpm.

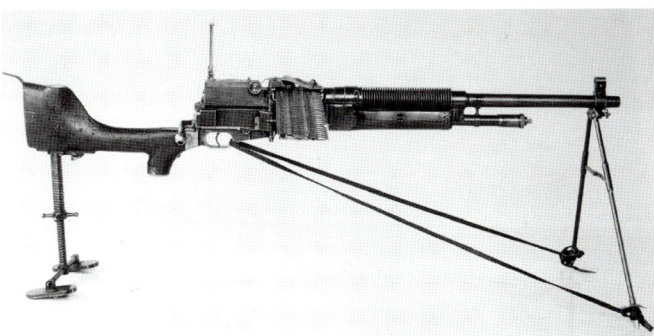

The Hotchkiss M1909 Light Machine Gun (also called the Hotchkiss MKI, the Hotchkiss Portative, and the Benet-Mercie Machine Rifle). It was chambered in French 8mm Lebel, British .303, and US .30-06.

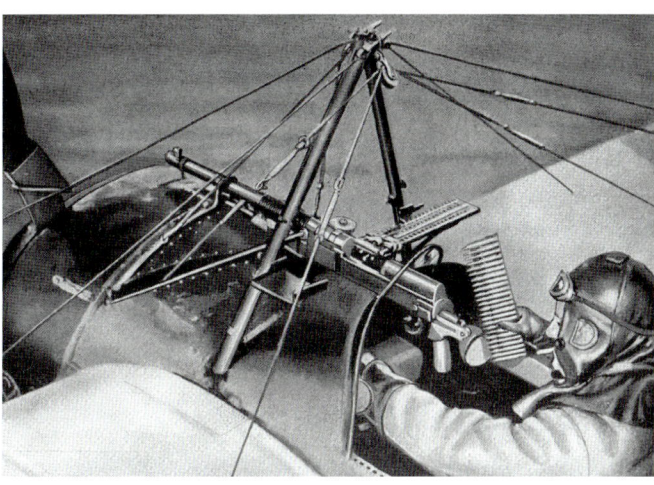

A French Morane with an unsynchronized Hotchkiss M1909 machine gun. At this point in the war the French used "deflector plates" to protect the propeller blades.

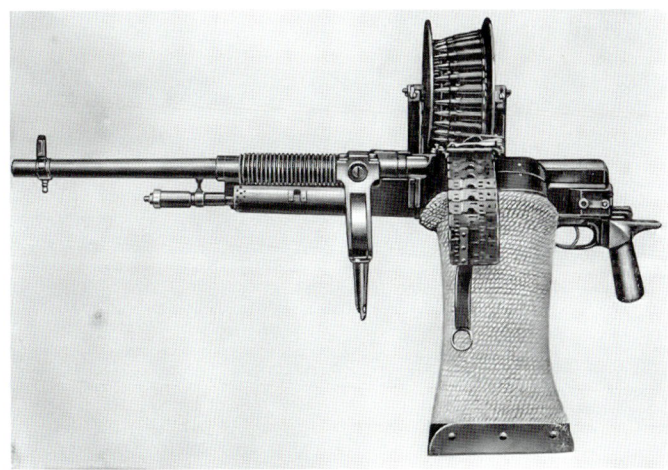

As an aircraft gun was fed by 30-round metal strips or via a cloth ammo belt on a large spool. Cyclic rate was 600 rpm.

Indian troops with a Hotchkiss Portative light machine gun, France 1918.

The Hotchkiss M1909 in strange mount to fire above the propeller aboard a Deperdussin TT.

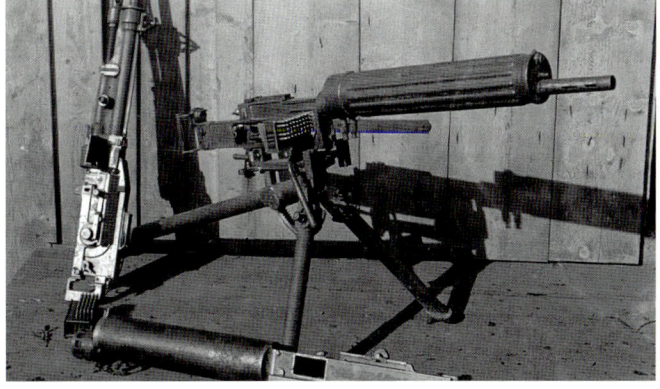

The Fiat-Revelli Modello 1914 water-cooled infantry gun. Note the unique feed system — a block of 6.5x52mm Carcano feed strips.

The Madsen light machine gun was created at a time when there was little thought given to the need for a light, man-portable automatic weapon. Adopted by the Danish Army in 1902, the Madsen would ultimately be sold to more than 30 countries, and was provided in 12 different calibers. The Imperial Russian Army purchased more than 1,200 Madsen guns (chambered in 7.62x54mmR) and used them for the first time in the Russo-Japanese War of 1904-1905. During WWI the Imperial Russian Air Service used Madsen guns on multiple aircraft as the observer's gun. The Madsen is recoil operated, and fires from an open bolt. Spent cartridges eject through the bottom of the receiver. It has a low rate of fire, about 450 rpm, and is fed by 25, 30, and 40-round magazines. Loaded weight is about 26 ½ pounds.

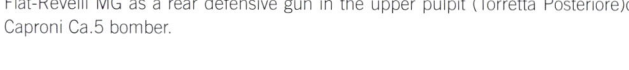

Fiat-Revelli MG as a rear defensive gun in the upper pulpit (Torretta Posteriore) on a Caproni Ca.5 bomber.

Detail view of the FIAT-Revelli M1914 aircraft gun.

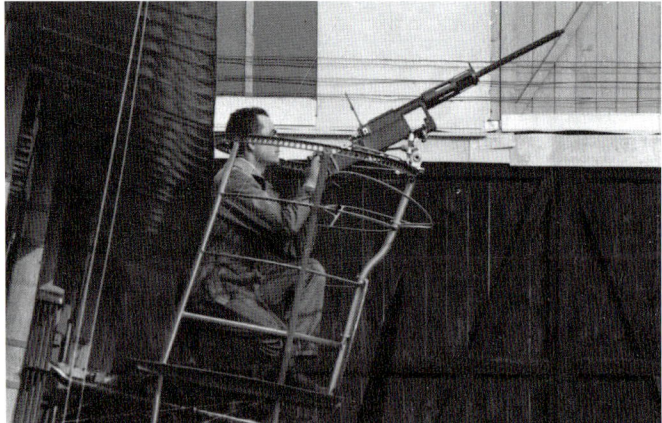

Russian airmen training with a Madsen LMG. The Imperial Russian Air Service made the greatest use of the Madsen of any WWI air force. (Via Kulikov)

The Madsen was used around the world in a wide variety of calibers. This M1925 Madsen (.303 British) is seen in Estonian service during the late 1920s.

A Madsen M/1902 clamped aboard a Russian Lebed XI. This gun has a 40-round magazine inserted. The Madsen continued to be used in the Imperial Russian Air Service until 1917.

A Madsen mounted in the topside gunner's position of an Il'ya Muromets bomber. Note the Mk. I Lewis ground gun mounted forward. (Via Kulikov)

THE SHAPE OF THINGS TO COME...

John Browning's air-cooled Model 1918 aircraft machine gun was not ready in time to see service in World War One. Even so, the weapon caught the attention of Aircraft Armament Board, particularly for its high rate of fire (1000 rpm). Ultimately the Browning .30 caliber, and the later .50 aircraft MGs, would become the standard US aircraft armament through the middle 1950s. In Europe, WWI aerial combatants searched intensively for weapons with a high cyclic rate. The Italians initially developed the fast-firing, double-barreled Villar-Perosa M1915 as an aircraft gun. Unfortunately, the Villa-Perosa's 9mm Glisenti rounds were too weak and too short-ranged to be of use in air fighting. With a cyclic rate of 1500 rpm (per gun) the VP drained its 25-round magazines exceptionally fast. When used as a ground weapon, the Villar-Perosa is considered one of the first successful submachine guns. In Germany, Carl Gast responded to the Fliegertruppen's request for greater firepower with the "Gast Maschinengewehr Modell 1917"—a twin barrel weapon (7.92x57mm) with an amazingly high cyclic rate of 1600 rpm (some reports quote as high as 1800 rpm). The Gast was fed by a pair of side-mounted drum magazines with 180 rounds contained in each. A few were tested in combat with good results during the autumn of 1918, but ultimately the Gast was too late to make a difference. Strangely, the Allied Control Commission did not learn of the Gast gun's existence until 1921.

Synchronization testing of an early Browning M1918 aircraft gun.

The Italian Villar-Perosa M1915, adapted from an aircraft weapon into an infantry gun.

The first Browning aircraft gun: the Model 1918.

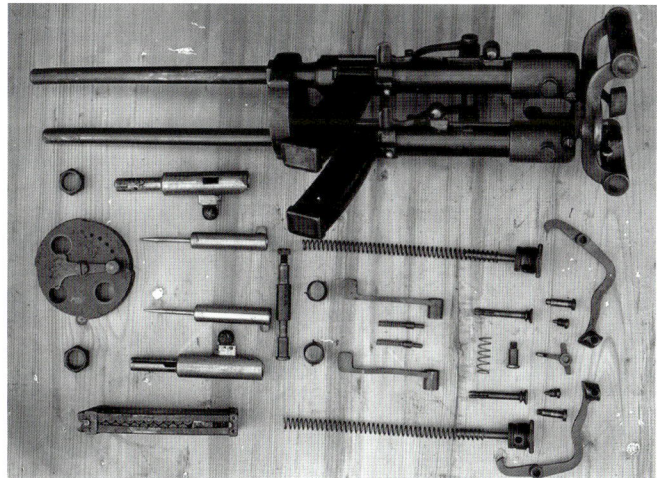
Details of the fast-firing (3000 rpm for the twin barrels) Villar-Perosa. The magazines only hold 25 rounds each.

The German secret weapon: The Gast Gun was fed by twin, side-mounted drums, each containing 180 rounds of 7.92mm ammunition. Total weight of the double-barreled Gast Gun (unloaded) was 60 pounds.

AERIAL GUNNERY TRAINING

An earth-bound US Air Service observer training with US Model 1918 Lewis guns on a duplex mount.

The official US Air Force history of the U.S. Air Service in World War I described the importance of advanced gunnery training for pilots and observers:

"Full courses in ground gunnery, including courses in deflection, were being carried on along with flying training at all principal schools. The camera gun was also extensively used in combat and other practice maneuvers, and constant shooting practice, both ground and aerial, was given to all pilots in squadrons at the front."

U.S. Air Service leaders concluded there was no substitute for combat experience:
"Fortunately, there were among the pilots some who had served with the Lafayette Escadrille and their experience in war was invaluable in teaching our new pilots, who had much to learn. The very best of schoolwork cannot give a pilot the atmosphere and feeling of the front—schooling cannot impress upon the students the relative importance of vision in the air, aerial gunnery, formation flying and fighting, and aerobatics."

US airmen in training at the aerial gunnery school at North Island, California in September 1918. In the foreground is a standard infantry Lewis gun with its buttstock replaced by a spade grip. In the center is a Marlin Model 1918 aircraft MG on a pilot trainer. The third gun in line is a US Model 1918 Lewis aircraft MG.

A rear view of the firing line and targets at the US Air Service aerial gunnery school.

The Hythe Mark III Gun Camera, designed to approximate the size, weight, and handling of the Lewis Gun.

GUNNERY TRAINING

Aircraft models played a vital role in aerial (and AA) gunnery training in World War One, as demonstrated by this British Vickers gun training unit in France.

Machine guns were in short supply: USMC observers get the feel for their new job using wooden dummy guns that approximate the Lewis MG.

The pilot's seat: The US Air Service aerial gunnery training school developed this device to simulate firing from the pilot's position, and equipped it with a Marlin M1918 aircraft MG.

A USMC observer training with a Model 1918 Aircraft Lewis MG (made by Savage Arms). The canvas bag on the right side of the gun captures the spent .30-06 casings. Note the "ring-post-and-bead" sights.

British and American observers train with the Lewis MKI in France during 1918. Mounted on simple tripods, the guns are equipped with 97-round drum magazines.

America's early airmen frequently began their gunnery training with trap-shooting. In this case these recruits use Winchester Model 1897 shotguns equipped with a special ring sight.

All sorts of firearms were used in aerial gunnery training, including pistols and rifles - like this 8mm Berthier Mle 1892 carbine, seen in France during the spring of 1918.

American aircrews gained much from experienced French and British instructors. Here a Royal Flying Corps veteran provides advice for a fledgling US air gunner in England during the spring of 1918.

French observers train in realistic positions while suspended in unique aircraft bodies. This appears to be an academic study hall coupled with a measure of practical experience. The man in the foreground handles a "stripped" MKI Lewis gun.

Aerial gunners must be intimately familiar with their weapons. The guns in this classroom are the US Model 1917 ground type Lewis (left) equipped with a spade grip, and a Colt-Browning M1895 MG (right). Georgia Tech School of Military Aeronautics, June 1918.

Learning to handle a US Model 1917 ground type Lewis gun by feel and memory, at the US School of Military Aeronautics at the University of California, Berkeley.

Wooden dummy guns continued to be used even into advanced training in France. Note the hand-cranked apparatus to give the target model wobbling flight characteristics.

A Winchester Model 1897 pump shotgun attached to a Scarff mount during training at Selfridge Field, Michigan during 1918.

US Air Service men training with Winchester Model 1911 SL (self-loading) shotguns at Issoudun, France during April 1918.

British and American observers learn the joys of loading 97-round Lewis gun drum magazines. A fully loaded 97-round drum weighed about 7.5 pounds and had a sturdy leather handle at the top to aid in handling.

GUNNERY TRAINING

The Hythe Mark III Gun Camera snapped a photo for each pull of the trigger. The images were reviewed to determine if the trainee was correctly tracking the target.

A Hythe Mark III Gun Camera set up to assess the pilot's performance in firing forward.

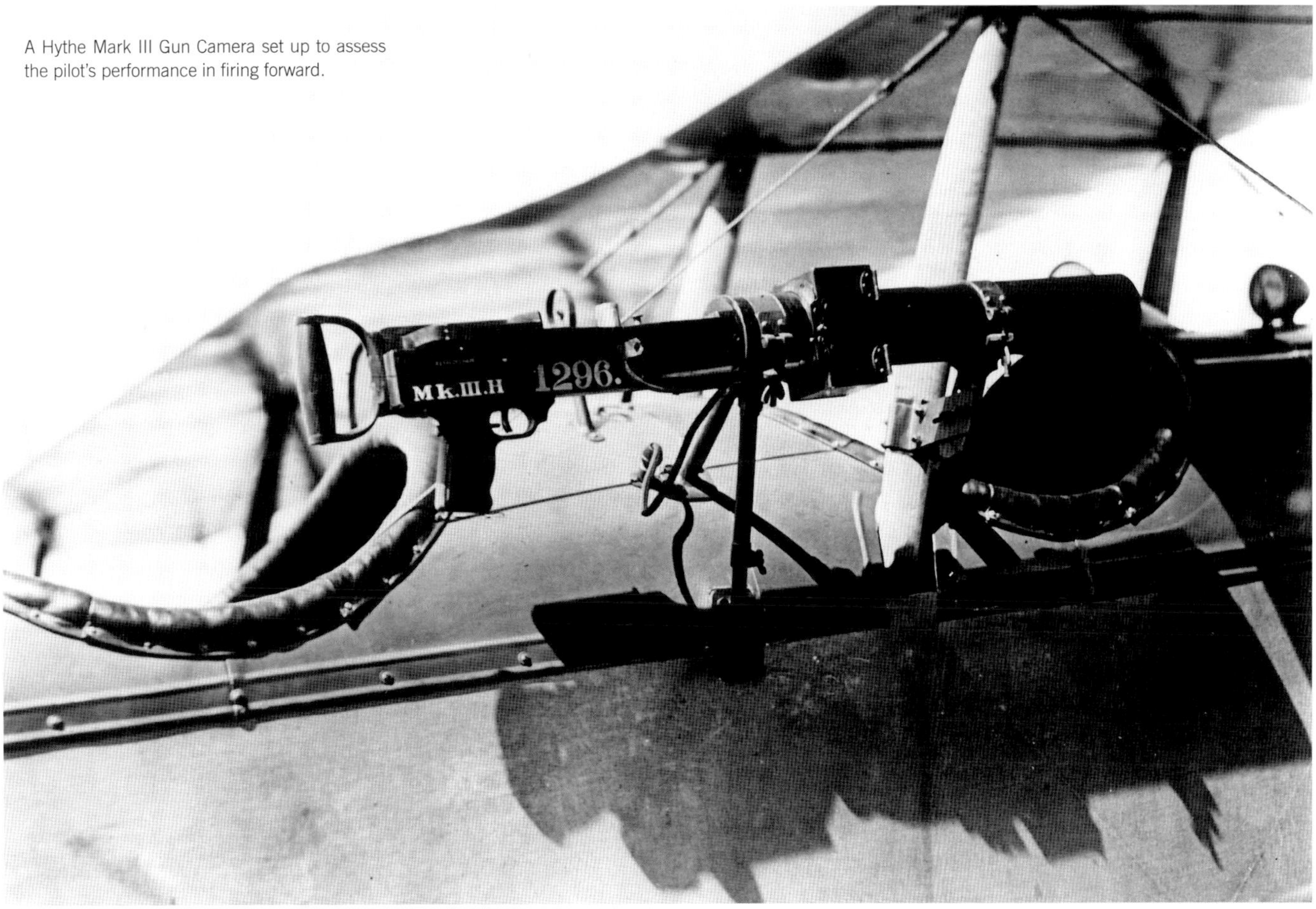

FORWARD FIRING GUNS
THE ALLIES

Instruction for the fledgling US Army Air Service: A French officer points out salient points of the Nieuport 17, fitted with the British Vickers MkI* MG. Note the blast deflector installed to protect the cowling and prop from damage. The projection above the muzzle is part of the French Alkan-Hamy synchronizing gear.

The Nieuport 17 featured a single Vickers MG (in this case a US Colt-made gun), using the French Alkan-Hamy synchronizing gear. The Nieuport was small aircraft, and the Vickers gun took up considerable space atop its 110 hp Le Rhone 9J engine. This example is seen in the USA (Hampton, Virginia) during June 1917.

This view shows the feed channel for the Vickers' disintegrating link ammunition belt. Spent casings were ejected below the breech and fell into their own discharge chute. Earlier Vickers mountings used "roll on — roll off" spools for the .303 cloth ammunition belts, travelling from right to left.

Inspecting a lineup of Nieuport 17 fighters equipped with Vickers MkI* guns and fitted with Alkan-Hamy synchronizing gear.

In addition to the synchronized Vickers gun, many later Nieuports (like this Type 23) carried a Lewis gun on the top wing. This stripped MkI Lewis (on a twin pylon mount) has no spade grip but uses an extended pistol grip.

Nieuport 17 with a single synchronized Vickers MkI*. The blast deflector can be clearly seen extending beneath the muzzle.

Nieuport 27 with a port-fuselage mounted Vickers gun.

A heavily armed Nieuport 17: A rare top wing mount featuring twin Lewis guns in addition to the synchronized Vickers. The twin Lewis and Vickers combination weighed about 64 pounds for the guns without ammunition — a considerable load for the 827-pound (empty) Nieuport.

A Sopwith Baby floatplane, equipped with a single Lewis gun firing above the propeller arc.

An early Nieuport 17 with a large spinner and a single Lewis gun mounted on the top wing.

The extremely narrow fuselage of the Nieuport 28 required that the twin Vickers guns were offset to the port side. These aircraft are part of the US 95th Aero Squadron.

Lieutenant Eddie Rickenbacker of the 94th Aero Squadron, seated in a Nieuport 28. Rickenbacker scored his first six victories in the Nieuport. Note the offset arrangement of the twin Vickers guns.

An early example of the Nieuport 28, featuring a single Vickers gun offset to port. Some pilots preferred a single gun arrangement to save weight.

A good view of the pilot's Vickers gun mounted on a Breguet 14 of the US 96th Aero Squadron. Also note the small metal shield (upper right) protecting the observer from metal links from the disintegrating ammo belt as well as spent cartridges ejected into the slipstream.

French ace Georges Guynemer (54 victories) aboard his SPAD S.VII "Vieux Charles". The SPAD S.VII carried a single Vickers gun, many of the early SPADs using the roll-on-roll-off spooling system for the cloth ammunition belts that was prone to jamming.

The forward-firing Vickers of a Breguet 14 A2. Note that the blast deflector has been mounted to the right to protect the fuselage and cowling. This is M1915 ground gun, made in the USA by Colt, and converted by the French for aerial use.

The Breguet 14's Vickers gun was mounted in a completely exposed position. Links from the disintegrating ammunition belt, along with spent cartridges were discharged into the airstream on the port side — necessitating the small metal shield (mounted just forward of the rear seat) designed to protect the observer from flying metal.

The Morane-Saulnier Type N used an unsynchronized Hotchkiss M1909 light machine gun (fed by 30-round metal strips). The propeller blades were "protected" by metal wedges designed to deflect the rounds that struck them.

SE5as in the Arras area during April 1918. These aircraft carry MkII Lewis guns on the early type of Foster mount for the top wing. A single Vickers MG is mounted to the left of fuselage (with "CC gear" for synchronization), with the gun's breech extending slightly into the cockpit.

The Royal Aircraft Factory SE5a was compact and maneuverable. The Lewis gun on a Foster mount on the top wing (in this case a Mk II Lewis) was able to fire upwards at an angle. Experienced pilots found this technique effective in attacking enemy aircraft from below in their blind spot.

The rare SPAD S.XII that featured an engine-mounted 37mm "Semi-Automatique Moteur Canon" (SAMC) built by Puteaux. Twelve 37mm rounds were carried. The cannon fired through the Hispano-Suiza engine's propeller shaft, ultimately proved difficult to use. The pilot reloaded the cannon by hand and the cockpit filled with gun smoke after each shot. A single Vickers gun was mounted on the starboard side of the nose.

The business end of the SPAD XIII and its twin Vickers guns, with Lt Eddie Rickenbacker in the pilot's seat. An alignment bar connects the two MGs, with a particularly large ring sight mounted to the pilot's right. Note the blast shields below the muzzles of these British-made MkI guns.

Armed with a single synchronized Vickers, the SPAD S.VII was considered a better gun platform than the more maneuverable Nieuport fighters.

FORWARD FIRING GUNS

Twin Colt-made Vickers aboard a US Army Air Service SPAD XIII. The US-built Vickers MGs feature an extra pair of cooling vents near the front plate.

French Sergeant Noof ready for take-off in his SPAD XIII during September 1918. A Colt-made Vickers MG can be seen on the cowling.

Sopwith Camel 2F.1 configured as a home-defense night fighter. One Vickers gun is fitted with a large ring sight, and a Lewis gun is mounted above the wing. The Lewis was often used at night to fire upwards at German Zeppelins or bombers. Muzzle flashes, particularly from the forward Vickers, were damaging to the pilot's night sight.

The Airco DH.5's was one of the first British aircraft to use the Constantinesco synchronization gear ("CC gear") for its single Vickers gun. The "back-staggered" wings of the Airco DH.5 gave the pilot much better forward vision, and this was thought to provide for more accurate shooting. Unfortunately, the poor aerial performance of the DH.5 negated any of these potential benefits.

The Sopwith Pup had twice the maneuverability of its normal opponent, the Albatross DIII, but only half the firepower, with a single Vickers MG.

The Sopwith Snipe was not particularly fast, but it was much easier to handle than the earlier Camel. The Snipe also featured better forward vision and was considered a better gun platform for its twin Vickers.

The Sopwith 1 ½ Strutter was the first British aircraft to enter service with a synchronized Vickers gun. Early Strutters used either the Vickers-Challenger synchronizing gear, or the Scarff-Dibovski gear. Later production models used the more reliable Ross or Sopwith-Kauper synchronizing gear.

Airco DH.4 with a single forward Vickers gun using Constantinesco synchronizing gear.

The Airco DH.9 bomber featured a Vickers MG synchronized to fire forward, and a single Lewis gun on a Scarff mount for the observer. Note the ejection port for spent casings immediately below the Vickers. Captain John Stevenson Stubbs (DFC AFC) brought down 11 German aircraft (including one balloon) while flying the DH.9.

Commander C. R. Samson's Nieuport 10, modified to carry an unmodified ground Lewis MG, mounted to fire upwards at an angle. Samson commanded No. 3 Squadron of the Royal Naval Air Service during the Dardanelles campaign of 1915. He holds a Webley 1913 (.455 SL) semi-auto pistol.

Three views of the tightly spaced twin Vickers MGs of the Sopwith Camel. All these aircraft flew with US 148th Aero Squadron.

A Camel of the US 148th Aero Squadron. The 5-inch ring front sight is attached by a circular clamp on the starboard Vickers gun.

Raoul Lufberry seated in the cramped confines of a Nieuport 17 cockpit. The Lewis gun is on a later twin-pylon mount (Type N65). The rear pylon was spring-loaded and would "break" in half to allow the Lewis to be pulled down for reloading.

The final development of the Curtiss triplane fighter, the experimental S-6. Note the strange twin Lewis gun mount. This arrangement appears to swivel, but it cannot be synchronized to fire through the propeller.

A cockpit view of twin Vickers guns. In later mountings like these, the port side Vickers was modified to load from the left, while the starboard Vickers loaded from the right (which was standard). Note the French-style extended cocking handles. Also, these Vickers do not have leather padding on the gun butts, which was standard in many Allied cockpits from 1917 onwards.

On the field with a Salmson 2 A.2 of the US 99th Aero Squadron.

Detail view of the Vickers gun mounted on the cowl of a Salmson 2 A.2 serving with the US 91st Aero Squadron.

The Salmson 2 A.2 featured a Vickers MG mounted on the cowl for the pilot, and a pair of Lewis guns for the observer. This Vickers is an American made gun, designated: "US Vickers Aircraft Machine Gun, Caliber .30, Model 1918".

A US Army Air Service Salmson 2 A.2 during synchronization tests for its twin Marlin M1918 MGs.

A detail view of the Salmson 2 A.2 nose. Note the 5-inch ring sight and the pilot's rear-view mirror.

A US-built DH.4 equipped with twin Marlin guns. The Marlin aircraft gun arrived in the late summer of 1918 and is most often seen as the synchronized MGs on US Army Air Service DH.4 and Salmson two-seaters. Pilot reports on the Marlin were favorable as the weapon had a higher cyclic rate than the Vickers and was less prone to freezing at higher altitudes.

The Italian Fiat-Revelli Modello 1914 (6.5x52mm) was a troublesome ground machine gun and a woeful aircraft weapon. It was fed by a bizarre "feed-strip box" (50 or 100 rounds), with a cyclic rate of as low as 400 rpm. Seen during tests in the USA during 1918.

A Fiat-Revelli Modello 1914 mounted on the top wing of an Italian S.A.M.L. S.2. Another M1914 was in a flexible mount for the observer.

A Russian Spad 7 captured by the Germans in November 1917. This aircraft carries a single Vickers machine gun. (Via Kulikov)

Alexander Sveshnikov in a Morane Saulnier H 1915. The Madsen LMG (chambered in 7.62x54mmR) fires up and over the propeller arc. The Madsen guns normally used 30 or 40-round magazines. (Via Kulikov)

A Russian Morane-Saulnier N monoplane fighter equipped with a Vickers guns provided by the British. (Via Kulikov)

The Imperial Russian Air Service operated this captured Halberstadt C. I, armed with a Colt-Browning M1895 MG (in 7.62x54mmR) synchronized and firing forward, a Lewis gun mounted on the top wing, and a German Parabellum in the observer's position. (Via Kulikov)

The Russian-designed Mosca MB bis fighter. Its Mk.I Lewis ground gun is mounted to fire upward at an angle. Note that the far end of the Lewis' radiator cooling sleeve has been removed. (Via Kulikov)

FORWARD FIRING GUNS
THE CENTRAL POWERS

Before the infamy: Hermann Goering was a 22-victory ace in WWI, holder of the Pour le Mérite, and commander of the "Flying Circus", Jagdgeschwader 1. He is seen here in the cockpit of a Fokker Dr.I triplane, behind twin LMG 08/15s. Note the ammunition feed channels, the sights, cocking handles, and the padded gun butts.

Fokker M.5K/MG set up for testing a Parabellum machine gun with early synchronization gear during April 1915. The Parabellum Model 1913 was rarely used in the synchronized/forward-firing role as the Germans opted for the LMG 08 and the LMG 08/15.

The synchronized gun: Anthony Fokker's synchronizing gear, coupled with his "Eindecker" monoplane design, constituted a major breakthrough in aerial armament. This Fokker E.II is armed with a LMG 08 that features a front "gate" sight.

Despite being bent and broken, this Eindecker shows off the mount of its synchronized LMG 08 Spandau machine gun — slightly offset to starboard. A 550-round belt of 7.92mm ammunition was carried.

The early Fokker pushrod control synchronizing gear had its share of problems, primarily due to the stiffness of the linkages—resulting in broken propellers and crashed aircraft.

Although primitive, the Eindecker's synchronized LMG 08 gave the Fliegertruppen a significant advantage over their opponents, creating the "Fokker Scourge" of the second half of 1915.

The E.IV was the final variant of the Eindeckers and early attempts were made to equip the E.IV with triple LMG 08 MGs — reportedly at the request of Max Immelmann. The triple gun configuration caused many problems with synchronizing gear, as well as adding considerable extra weight with the extra gun and ammunition.

The Eindecker E.IV with triple Spandau MGs. Although Immelmann is said to have used it successfully, standard production E.IVs were equipped with only two LMG 08s.

Anthony Fokker stands in the cockpit of his E.IV design. Note the twin guns and the ventilation holes cut in the cowl for the 14-cylinder Oberursel U.III engine. The guns of the E.IV were inclined slightly (15 degrees) and this was not popular with pilots.

The Austro-Hungarian Schwarzlose MG 16 mounted on a Fokker Eindekker.

An Eindecker fitted with a Parabellum Model 1913 MG. The combination of the Parabellum and the early synchronizing gear did not work very well and the LMG 08 became the standard synchronized forward gun. The firing button can be seen in the upper middle of the Eindecker's control column.

The highly effective Fokker D.VII. The D.VII was able to "hang" on its prop for a short time, and pilots used this technique to pour fire from their twin LMG 08/15s into the belly of their opponents flying above. During the summer of 1918 some problems were encountered when engine heat ignited phosphorus ammunition — forcing the D.VIIs to stop using incendiary ammo until the problem was resolved in a few weeks time.

High-tech in 1918: To take advantage of the Fokker D.VII's nearly 20,000-foot service ceiling, this example is equipped with a liquid oxygen respirator. Note the details of the LMG 08/15s — link discharge pipe, cocking handles, and padded gun butts.

Fokker E.V parasol monoplane (later modified and designed D.VIII) was the last Fokker design to see combat with the German Army Air Service. Armament was a pair of LMG 08/15 MGs.

The Fokker E.V, sometimes called "The Flying Razor" by Allied pilots. Ammunition load for the LMG 08/15 MGs was up to 500 rounds per gun. Some E.V's were equipped with ammunition counters mounted on the gun butts.

A pre-production Fokker Triplane, designated F.I (FI 102/17). Manfred Richthofen flew this aircraft at the beginning of September 1917 and downed two enemy planes within two days — leading to his recommendation that fighter Jastas should be equipped with the Triplane as soon possible. Lt. Kurt Wolff was shot down and killed in this aircraft on September 15, 1917.

The Fokker Dr.I offered incredible maneuverability as well as providing a highly stable gun platform for its twin LMG 08/15 MGs. However, a significant negative was the tight positioning of the machine guns to the cockpit, coupled with inadequate padding of the gun butts, leading to serious head injuries during crash landings. This Dr.I was the first Triplane to be captured intact by the Allies (on January 13, 1918).

A Dr.I pilot prepares for battle. Twin LMG 08/15s wait to be turned loose on the enemy.

Details of the gun installation on a Fokker D.VII. Note the ammunition feed channel and the gun cocking handles.

The LVG C.VI carried up to 1000 rounds for its forward-firing LMG 08/15. The opening below the strut is the ejection port for spent casings.

Tiny fighter with a big bite: Twin Spandaus mounted on the SSW D.IV. The metal chute on the port side gun carries the spent ammunition belt.

Lt. Hartmuth Baldamus, (18 victories) killed in an air collision with a Nieuport during April 1917. Note the bowl-style cover over the spent casing ejection port.

Lt. Pfeifer aboard an Albatross D.II. From the start, their twin Spandau MGs gave Albatross fighters a distinct firepower advantage over their Allied opponents.

Charging the guns of an Albatross fighter. It is rare to see a pilot wearing the Model 1916 Stahlhelm.

An excellent view of the LMG 08/15s mounted on an Albatross D.III, captured near Aux-le-Chateau, and on its way to a British aviation depot. March 1917.

The twin Spandau MGs of the Pfalz D.IIIa. This later version of the Pfalz fighter moved the guns up from within the fuselage to give the pilot access in case of a jam.

Captive Albatross: A detail view of an Albatross D.V cockpit. Note the small windscreen, the rear-view mirror, and the bowl-shaped cover for the spent shell casing ejection port. This aircraft was brought down in British territory during early 1918.

The Black Knight: Eduard Ritter von Schleich scored 29 of his 35 total victories in an Albatross D.V. Note the Bavarian lion motif, the ace's personal marking.

The sad remains of an Albatross D.III: With its wings removed, details of the Austro-Daimler 200hp 6-cylinder water-cooled in-line engine and the LMG 08/15 guns are easily seen.

A detail view of the port gun of a Pfalz D.IIIa brought down by British ground fire during April 1918.

The Fokker D.II was hoped to maintain the "Fokker Scourge" over the Western Front, but unfortunately the biplane offered little more performance than the Eindecker. A single Spandau was fitted.

A late-production Pfalz D.VII, armed with a pair of LMG 08/15 MGs. Capable of 120 mph, the little Pfalz were used mostly for evaluation purposes late in the war.

The forward gun: Most German two-seaters carried a single synchronized LMG 08/15 firing forward, as on this LVG C.VI. As the war progressed, strafing became more and more important, and the opportunity to shoot down Allied aircraft led to a handful of "two-seater" aces.

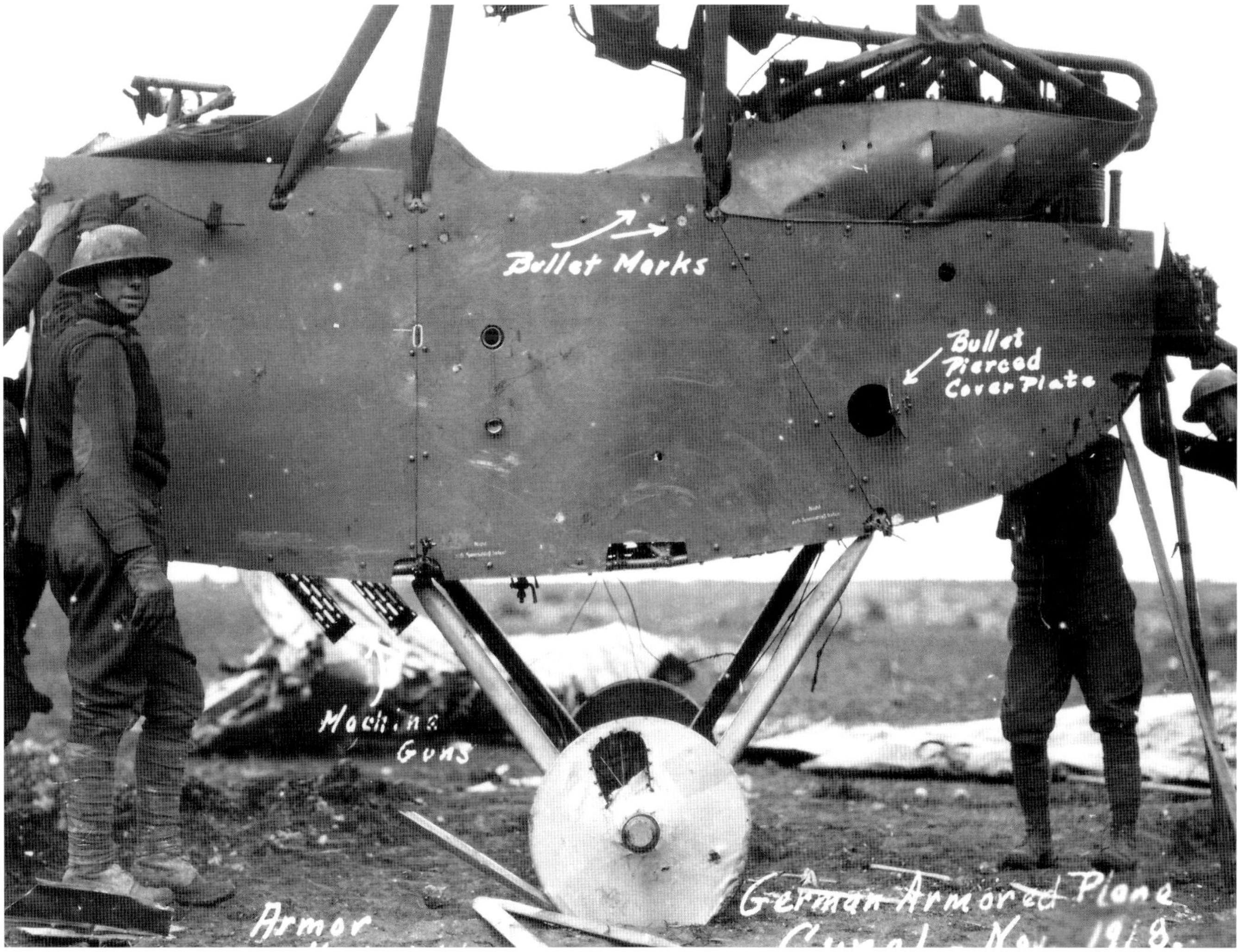

American troops inspect the remains of a downed AEG J.1, brought down near Cunel, France during October 1918. This was an armored aircraft, its fuselage protected by 5mm of armor plate. Twin Spandau MGs were mounted in the floor of rear cockpit, angled downward for strafing and operated by the observer.

OBSERVER'S GUNS
THE ALLIES

The twin Lewis guns of a Breguet 14. This aircraft is from the US 96th Aero Squadron. The Lewis guns are French-built by Darne, carried in a TO-3 "tourelle" mount. Note the field modified skeletal pistol grip added to the port side gun just below the gas cylinder.

Breguet 14 of the US 96th Aero Squadron. These were the first American-crewed bombers in action.

French and American Breguet 14 crews pose at an advanced flight training center in France during the spring of 1918. Note that the Breguet in the background carries a Lewis gun on the top wing in double-pylon mount.

A French instructor points out details of the twin Lewis guns (French-built Darne) carried in a TO-3 "tourelle" mount on a Breguet 14.

A French Breguet 14 that returned safely after being hit by AA fire over German lines.

The pedestrian SPAD 16 A2. A few were used by American squadrons for recon duties in the latter part of 1918. This particular aircraft was flown by General Billy Mitchell, and has a Lewis Mk.I mounted in the rear cockpit. It is now preserved in the Smithsonian National Air & Space Museum.

A Nieuport 12 carrying a pair of Lewis guns. The gun in the rear cockpit is mounted to a Eteve ring (also called the "Nieuport ring"). The Nieuport 12 was flown by French and British squadrons, and in some cases remained in service until the summer of 1917.

A Farman F.40 armed with a spool-fed Hotchkiss M1909 machine gun and launch tubes for Le Prieur rockets. US AEF commander General John Pershing is seen at the right.

The French Hotchkiss Mle 1914 MG is rarely seen mounted on aircraft. Although it was an early air-cooled design, the gun itself weighs a hefty 52 pounds, and its 30-round metal feed strips make it awkward to load and fire in the tight space of this Voisin 8 cockpit.

A French Voisin LA forced down in German territory. It is armed with a Hotchkiss M1909 MG.

A Colt-Browning M1895 mounted on a simple pintle aboard a Russian Voisin LA. (Via Kulikov)

The Russians used some modified Vickers MGs as "flexible" guns for observers. The Vickers aboard this Voisin LA has had its cooling jacket drained of water and little other modification. It is tied to a cockpit strut for takeoff. Note the large ammunition canister. (Via Kulikov)

A Russian Voisin LA equipped with a "stripped" Vickers New Light Model 1906, with its water jacket cut away. To the right is a drum for the MG's 250-round canvas belt. The pan-like object below the barrel is a spent casing collector, to keep the hot brass from falling on the pilot's head! (Via Kulikov)

A Vickers equipped Sikorsky S-16. (Via Kulikov)

A Colt Browning M1895 (in 7.62x54mmR) on a Russian Voisin LA, mounted to fire forward over the pilot's position. (Via Kulikov)

The Imperial Russian Air Service badly needed machine guns, and although the Colt-Browning M1895 was not well-suited to the role as an aircraft gun, the Russians found ways to make it work. The M1895 on this Lebed XII is fed by a locally made ammunition belt drum. Also note the metal box attached to the right side to collect spent casings. (Via Kulikov)

Pusher aircraft like this Farman F.40 offered gunners an excellent forward view, while the rear of the aircraft was nearly indefensible. In this case, a strip-fed Hotchkiss M1909 is mounted for the pilot's use, while a spool-fed Colt-Browning M1895 gun (on a Nieuport ring) can fire forward or over the top wing to the rear.

A Breguet BM 4 bomber with a forward mounted M1909 Hotchkiss MG. This weapon is belt fed via a large spool.

The Russians received only a small number of the Lewis guns they requested. This Lewis Mk.I protects the tail of a massive Il'ya Murometz bomber. (Via Kulikov)

A Colt-Browning M1895 mounted in the front cockpit of a Russian Farman HF.27 during the winter of 1917. (Via Kulikov)

Not for the squeamish: A Colt-Browning M1895 mounted on the top wing to cover the tail of this Caudron G.4. The gunner demonstrates how he steadies his firing position by grasping one of the fuselage support struts.

Lewis guns set up to fire fore and aft on a Caudron G.4.

The "Brisfit": The Bristol F.2B was a deadly two-seat fighter, with a single synchronized Vickers firing forward and a pair of Lewis guns in the rear. Some gunners opted for a single Lewis, as the hefty twin-gun Scarff mount presented a physical challenge to swing about at altitude.

A US-built DH.4 armed with twin Marlin and Lewis guns.

A US Army Air Service DH.4 in France. Note the details on the US .30 caliber Model 1918 Lewis aircraft gun (made by Savage) and its attachment to the Scarff mount. Also note the improvised padding added to the butts of the Marlin guns to protect the pilot's head.

OBSERVER'S GUNS

DH.4 lovely "Juanita" shows off her all-American armament: Twin US M1918 Lewis guns with Norman vane sights and distinct US-style muzzle brakes.

The American DH.4: The first DH.4 completed in the USA, this aircraft carries a pair of synchronized Marlin aircraft machine guns. The twin Lewis guns are equipped with Norman vane front sights.

A Sopwith 1 ½ Strutter with a Mk.II Lewis (RFC pattern) equipped with a Norman vane sight. Note the details on the synchronized Vickers Mk.I* and its large ring sight.

The observer of this Sopwith 1 ½ Strutter strikes an aggressive pose with his Mk.II Lewis.

American made machine guns in France 1918: A pair of Savage-made M1918 Lewis aircraft guns (with a Norman vane sight) and twin Model 1917 Marlin aircraft MGs using CC synchronizing gear.

A war captured in moving pictures: A cine camera mounted in the observer's position of a DH.9 with the US 148th Aero Squadron. The aircraft is not unarmed though, as evidenced by the Vickers gun beside the pilot's position.

American DH.4 crews prepare for a mission in France during the autumn of 1918. The Lewis gun is a US M1918 aircraft gun (.30 caliber). Twin Marlin guns are synchronized for use by the pilot.

The christening of the "Langley", the first Handley Page O/400 made in America. Twin US M1918 Lewis guns are carried in the nose.

Lewis gun positions on a Handley Page O/400 bomber based at Dunkirk during April, 1918.

A giant with folded wings: the Lewis gun in the nose turret appears rather puny against the backdrop of the massive Handley Page O/400.

The nose turret of a crashed Caudron R.11 escort fighter. Both Lewis guns have spent casing collector bags fitted and several 97-round magazines can be seen in the wreck.

One gunner, many Lewis guns: The gunner on this F.E.2b demonstrates the physical difficulties of covering the tail of a pusher aircraft.

A British F.E.2a brought down behind German lines during 1916. A Lewis Mk.II is mounted in the front cockpit.

An Italian S.A.M.L. 2 equipped with a Fiat-Revelli Model 1914 for the observer, and another mounted on the top wing to fire above the propeller arc.

An Italian Pomilio PE. The observer's gun is a Fiat-Revelli Model 1914 aircraft gun.

A rare image of a Caproni Ca.5 bomber — a pair of Fiat-Revelli Model 1914 MGs (6.5mm) are mounted in the nose gunner's position.

A Madsen LMG in the observer's position aboard a Russian Morane-Saulnier Type L. The gun is an unmodified infantry weapon (retaining its bipod) and used without any aircraft mount. Crew: pilot-volunteer non-commissioned officer Stanislaw Jakubowski in front of the cabin and observer Praporshchik Vladimir Eremenko of the 16th corps aviatio detachment, autumn 1915.
(Via Kulikov)

A Schwarzlose M.7 infantry machine gun mounted on a captured Albatross B.II in service with the Imperial Russian Air Service. Note the large bag to capture spent ammunition casings. (Via Kulikov)

Russian observer with a British-made Mk.I Lewis in the rear seat of a Morane-Saulnier Type L. The front part of the Lewis' radiator casing has been removed and the gun is equipped with an infantry-type 47-round drum. Note the simple clamp and pedestal mount.
(Via Kulikov)

Twin Lewis guns are mounted in the nose gun position of this Italian Caproni Ca.4 triplane bomber. The Caproni could carry up to 3,200 pounds of bombs.

Two Fiat-Revelli Model 1914 MGs aboard an Italian S.I.A. 7.

Two images of Salmson 2 A.2 recon aircraft of the US 91st Aero Squadron. The Lewis guns are fitted with a Norman van sight. The photography equipment is a Kodak Aero Camera Model B1.

Twin Lewis guns aboard American Salmson 2 A.2s in France during late 1918.

Salmson 2 A.2s of the US 91st Aero Squadron.

Sea bird: An M1918 Lewis aboard a US-built Felixstowe F.5L flying boat.

Details of the nose turret and cockpit of a US-built Felixstowe F.5L flying boat.

Lewis gun ammunition storage in the nose turret of a US-built Felixstowe F.5L flying boat. The shelves to the left are for Lewis 97-round drums.

Flying boat gun: The forward Lewis gun position aboard a Curtiss H-16 "Large America" flying boat.

A M1918 Lewis in the nose turret of a US-built Felixstowe F.5L flying boat. These British designs were made in Philadelphia by the Naval Aircraft Factory.

An inside view of the nose of a F.5L flying boat showing storage for the Lewis gun.

By air, land, or sea — the Lewis was the prime defensive gun for Allied aircraft of all types. This example is mounted in the nose of a US Navy F.5L flying boat.

The French Letord Let. 7, reconnaissance bomber/night bomber. The Lewis gun in the nose is a standard Mk.I ground gun simply modified with a spade grip replacing its normal shoulder stock.

Mission briefing for the crew of a Royal Aircraft Factory R.E.8. The observer has a RFC pattern Mk.II Lewis.

A view of the gondola of a US Navy dirigible based in France during 1918. A standard Lewis Mk.I is mounted at the front of the car. Only the front portion of the radiator shroud is removed — a normal French practice.

OBSERVER'S GUNS
THE CENTRAL POWERS

The Parabellum: The German Model 1913 was second only to the Lewis gun as an air defense gun.

Early mounts for the Parabellum Model 1913 were often rather awkward, as on this Albatross B-I (where the observer sat in the forward seat). Note the box container for the 200-round ammunition belt.

Albatross C-1 with a Parabellum Model 1913 for the observer. Note the Mauser Karabiner KAR 98AZ to the fuselage. The KAR 98AZ was about six inches shorter than the standard Gewehr 98 rifle.

An AEG C.1. It's Parabellum MG is on a Schneider gun mount.

The eyes of the Kaiser's army: The observer's primary job was to locate the enemy, and the Parabellum MG was to help him return safely and deliver the information to those who need it.

The rear gunner didn't always fire to the rear. The Parabellum MG on this Albatross can fire forward at an angle that remains outside the propeller arc.

Totenkopf motif: The observer and his Parabellum MG aboard a LVG C.V.

The crew of an Albatross C.XII waits for their aircraft to be readied. Note the LMG 08/15 mounted on the starboard side of the pilot's position.

DFW C.V on the Piave front in Italy. The gun is a Parabellum Model 1913.

The armor-plated (5mm) AEG J.1 ground attack aircraft. In addition to the Parabellum defensive gun, the observer also operated a pair of downward-firing LMG 08/15s (mounted in the rear cockpit floor) for strafing.

The Roland C.II provided a fantastic field of fire around the upper portion of the aircraft, but the high fuselage coupled with the lower wing created a horrible blind spot from below.

An excellent view of the Parabellum Model 1913 MG with a 200-round belt spool. The Model 1916 helmet perfectly fits the persona, and the job, of the "Infanterieflieger" gunner.

An Albatross C.V equipped with a Parabellum Model 1913. The gun is attached with a standard "fork-and-clamp" mount.

The enemy's view of the Parabellum Model 1913. A support bar is attached from the ammunition spool to the gun's front plate, to keep the ammo belt feeding at a 90-degree angle. Note the details of the simple ring front sight.

AEG C.IV with its Parabellum mounted on a horseshoe-shaped rail instead of a ring. The observer taps on an early radio transmitter.

Arriving in the summer of 1918, the Halberstadt C.V was fast and maneuverable for a two-seater. A Model 1913/17 MG is mounted on a late-model cast metal gun ring with an excellent field of fire.

A Schwarzlose MG-16 machine gun mounted on a Brandenburg C.1. This version of Schwarzlose featured a cyclic rate of 800 rpm.

A Brandenburg C.1(Ph) with a Schwarzlose MG-16 aircraft gun for the observer, and a VK Type II gun cannister mounted on the top wing. Note the crate of messenger pigeons.

A cold and lonely job: A good view of a Parabellum Model 1913 with its 200-round ammunition belt spool. An LMG 08 is visible just forward of the pilot's position.

The Halberstadt CL.II provided one the finest observer gun platforms of any WWI aircraft. The gunner for "Brunhilde" has an optical sight fitted to his Parabellum. Note the box of grenades and the band of flares fitted to the fuselage.

A Halberstadt CL.II showing its distinctive rear gun ring. Note the fuselage-mounted box of flares and attached Hebel Model 1894 flare pistol.

The rear gun position of the Halberstadt CL.II: The top and bottom images show a Parabellum Model 1913/17, and the center image shows the earlier Model 1913.

The AGO C.1 pusher reconnaissance aircraft. The pusher design gave the forward gunner an excellent field of fire. A single Parabellum Model 1913 was mounted in the nose.

This AGO C.1 gunner demonstrates the full field of fire with his Bergmann MG 15 a.A. This weapon is fitted with a "gate"-style front sight.

An LVG C.VI armed with a captured Lewis gun for the observer. The Lewis was very popular with the Germans, and many guns and magazines were captured and used. This example appears to be a modified infantry gun, retaining its original butt stock.

The DFW C.V was highly maneuverable, and a good pilot could out-fly most of the Allied fighters of 1917 — with a sting in the tail. Here, armorers attach the Parabellum's 200-round ammunition belt spool.

A second view of the DFW C.V's rear gun position: Even though the weather on the ground is warm, the observer is dressed for the chill of higher altitudes.

A Parabellum on a tall pillar mount to fire above the propeller arc. The gunner would have to stand up in this scenario, grasping the leg of the tripod with his off hand to remain upright.

This Euler C1 has a Bergmann MG15n.A. (7.92x57mm) mounted on the top wing to fire above the propeller arc. The Bergmann is equipped with a "gate" front sight and a 200-round ammunition belt box. No spent shell collecting bag is fitted.

A Parabellum in the nose of a Friedrichshafen G.III bomber, brought down in France during early 1918. Two or three defensive guns were fitted, and the G.III carried up to 2,200 pounds of bombs.

Two Parabellum MGs cover the rear of this AEG G.II bomber. The guns are mounted on a rail around the rear cockpit.

Nose gunner on a Gotha G.V with a OIGEE optical sight. This LMG 13/17 is fitted with a recoil booster.

Gotha gunner in position. His LMG 13/17 is fitted with an optical sight, preferred by some gunners. Note his oxygen breathing tube.

Gotha G.V gunners: their LMG 13/17 guns have 200-round ammunition drums.

The front turret of the Gotha G.V offered an excellent field of fire for the gunner. The MG is a Parabellum Model 1913/17. Note the 50 kg PuW bombs beneath the fuselage.

A good view of the nose gunner's position of an AEG bomber — the Parabellum attached to the ring with a "fork-and-clamp" mount. This aircraft was brought down and captured at Villacoublay, France during June 1918.

A Parabellum in the nose position of an AEG G.II bomber. Part of Manfred von Richthofen's early career included serving as gunner aboard one of these aircraft.

BOMBS AND GRENADES

US trainees load Mark II 20-pound bombs aboard a Curtiss Jenny during stateside training in early 1918.

The first explosive aerial bomb, dropped from a Wright Brothers Model B in 1911.

A bomb sling — an early attempt at bomb release controlled by the pilot.

The 20-pound "Hales Bomb" (4.5 pounds of explosive), used in the September 1914 attack on the Zeppelin sheds near Cologne.

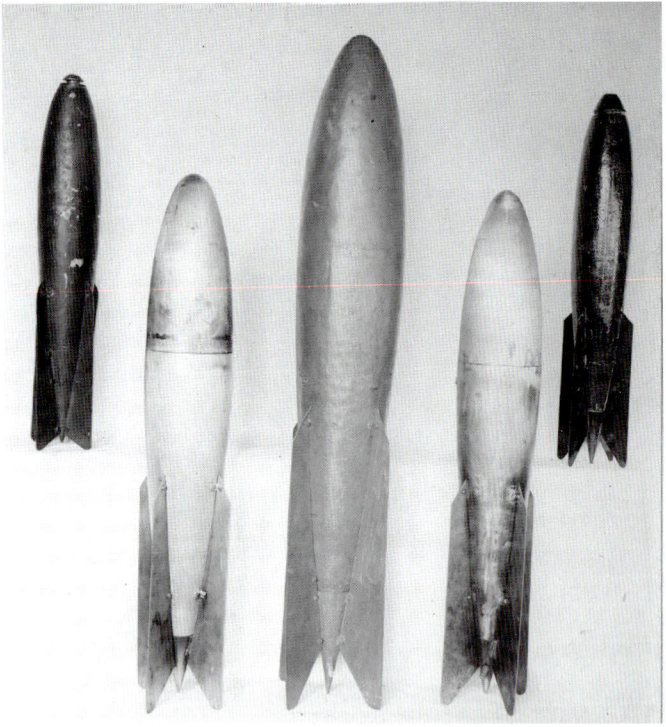
A selection of US practice bombs.

US bombs and incendiaries seen in late 1918.

A US Navy 250-pound bomb, carried by USN dirigibles.

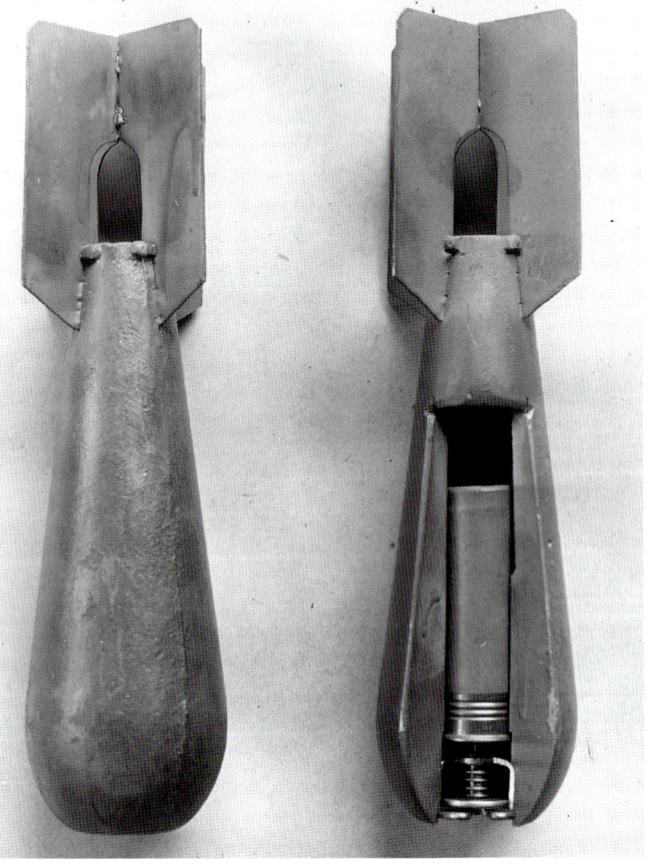
A US Navy practice bomb that used a 10-gauge shotgun shell to create a plume of white smoke.

Russian Air Service officer posing with a 25-pud (880 pound) bomb. This weighty WWI ordnance could be carried by the massive Il'ya Muromets II bomber.

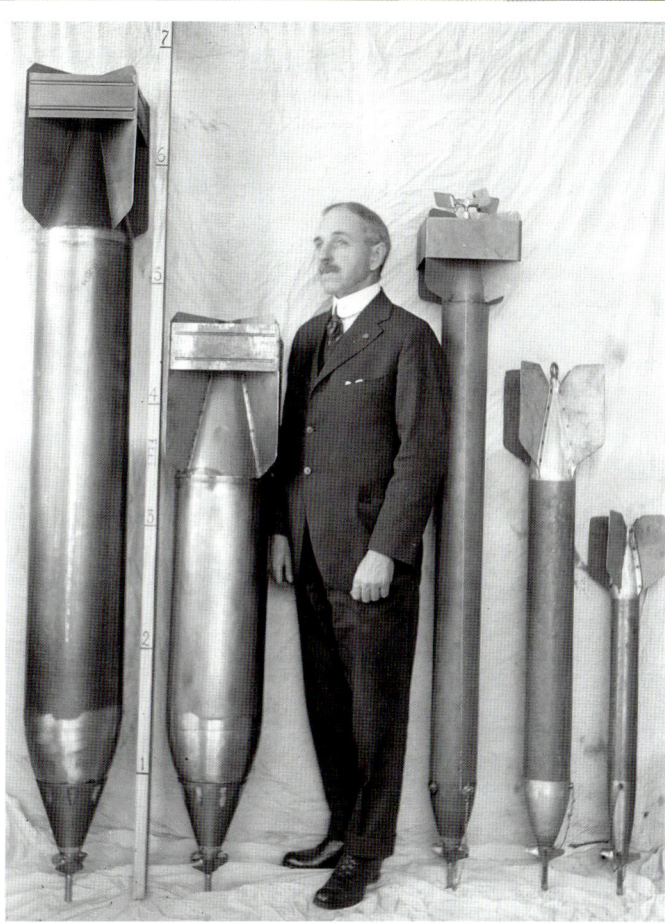

L.S. Clarke, head of the Autocar Company, posing with bombs he invented for the US military during 1918.

The US airman shows off a French smoke bomb (8.1 kg).

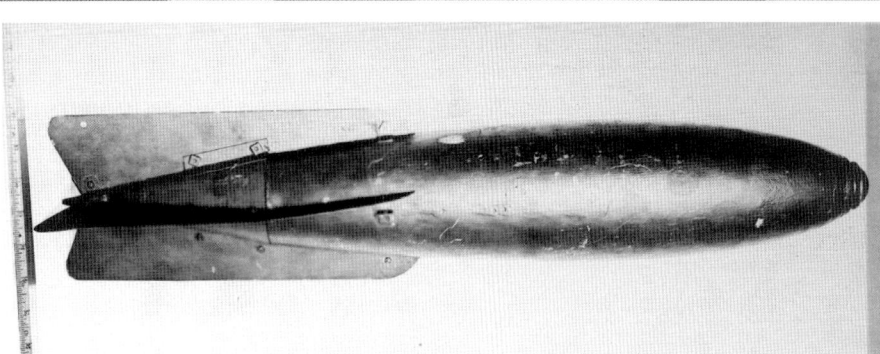

The US MKII 20-pound bomb.

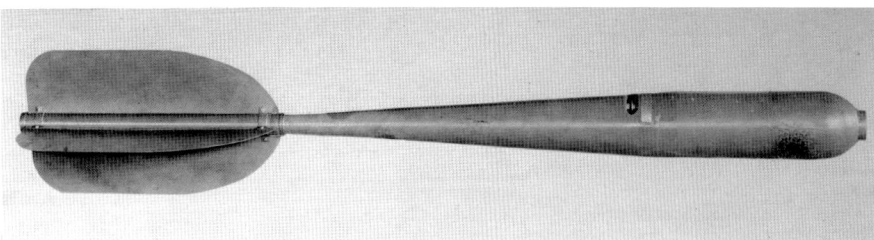

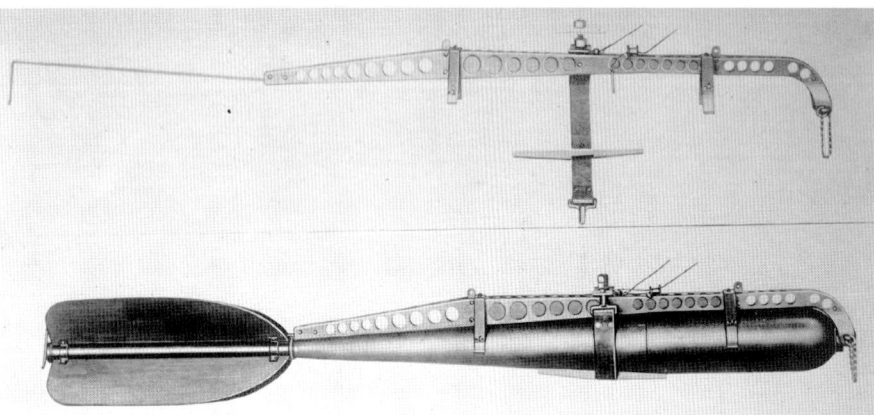

Three views of the small US "Barlow Bomb" (also called an "aerial torpedo" by its inventor) and its patented release mechanism. Barlow designed this particular device to explode slightly above ground to achieve better fragmentation effect. Almost 9,000 of these were made by the Marlin–Rockwell Corporation but the AEF cancelled the contract and the weapon was not used in combat.

Men of the US 96th Aero Squadron fusing bombs for their Breguet 14 bombers near Amanty, France during August 1918. The "115 Long Explosive Bomb" (20.2 kilograms total weight, carrying 12.2 kilograms of explosive) is seen to the right.

A DH.4 with a load of 20-pound bombs.

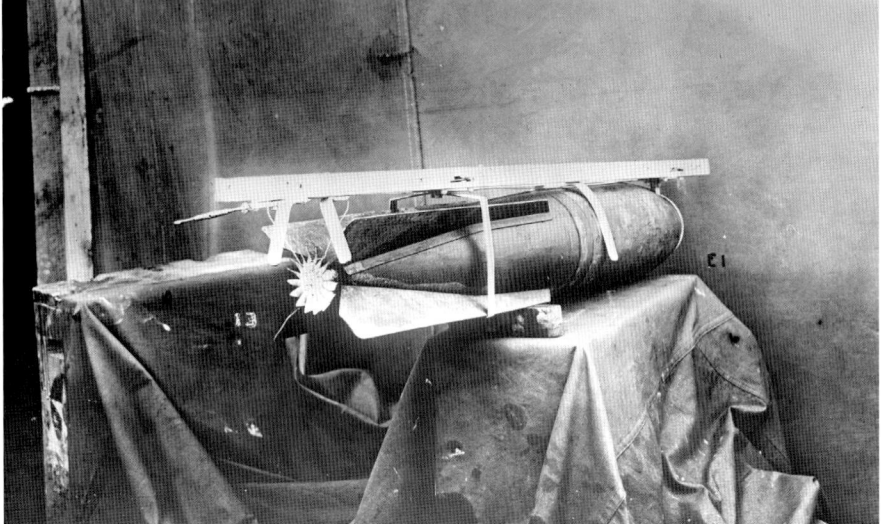

An unidentified bomb (possibly a converted artillery shell) on an improvised bomb rack destined for a Breguet 14.

The bomb and rack shown above, as fitted to a Breguet 14 A2 of the US 96th Aero Squadron

Bombing technology advanced rapidly as the war progressed. This bomb rack and release mechanism was designed by the Curtiss Aeroplane and Motor Corporation during late 1918.

Loading 20-pound practice bombs aboard a Curtiss JN-6BH "Jenny" bomber trainer at Langley Field (Hampton, Virginia) during 1918.

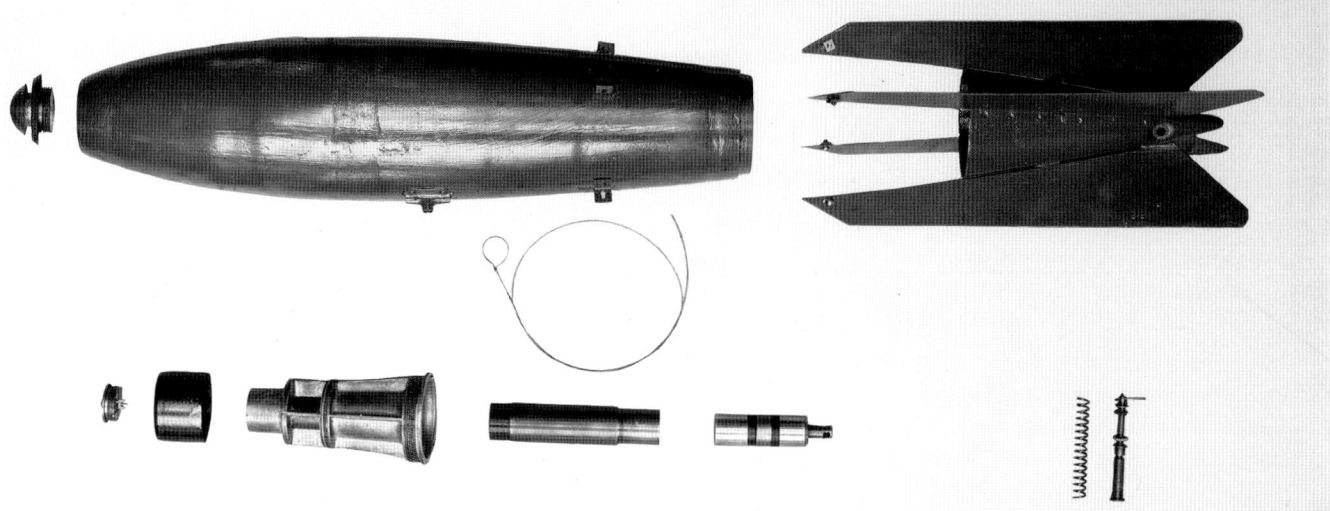

Details of the US Mark II 20-pound bomb made by the Marlin-Rockwell Company.

SPAD S.XIII fitted with a Cooper bomb rack and 20-pound Cooper bombs.

Reverse view of the Cooper bomb rack fitted to the SPAD S.XIII.

Salmson 2 A.2 with twin Cooper racks.

A pair of 250-pound bombs on the starboard rack of the US Navy C-1 Dirigible, late 1918.

British air crews prepare 112-pound bombs for an O/100 bomber based at Dunkirk during 1917.

Loading 1-pud (35.3 pound) bombs aboard an Imperial Russian Air Service Henri Farman F.22.

Nieuport 11 armed with Le Prieur rockets. These rockets were essentially air-to-air spears for use against observation balloons. Each La Prieur contained 200 grams of black powder - if the rocket's knife blade stuck in the balloon canvas the consequent flash of the powder ignited the enemy gas bag. Horribly inaccurate, the rockets maximum range was little more than 100 meters and also required a steep dive into the wind to whenever possible to produce better results.

A Farman F.40P armed with ten La Prieur rockets. The La Prieur projectiles were introduced during April 1916.

German troops pose with a wrecked Handley Page bomber near Lys, France. Its bomb load is scattered throughout the crash site.

Loading 20-pound Cooper bombs aboard an early production Armstrong Whitworth F.K.8.

German 4.7 liter incendiary (left) and a 12.5 kg Carbonit bomb (right).

German 12.5 kg PuW bombs.

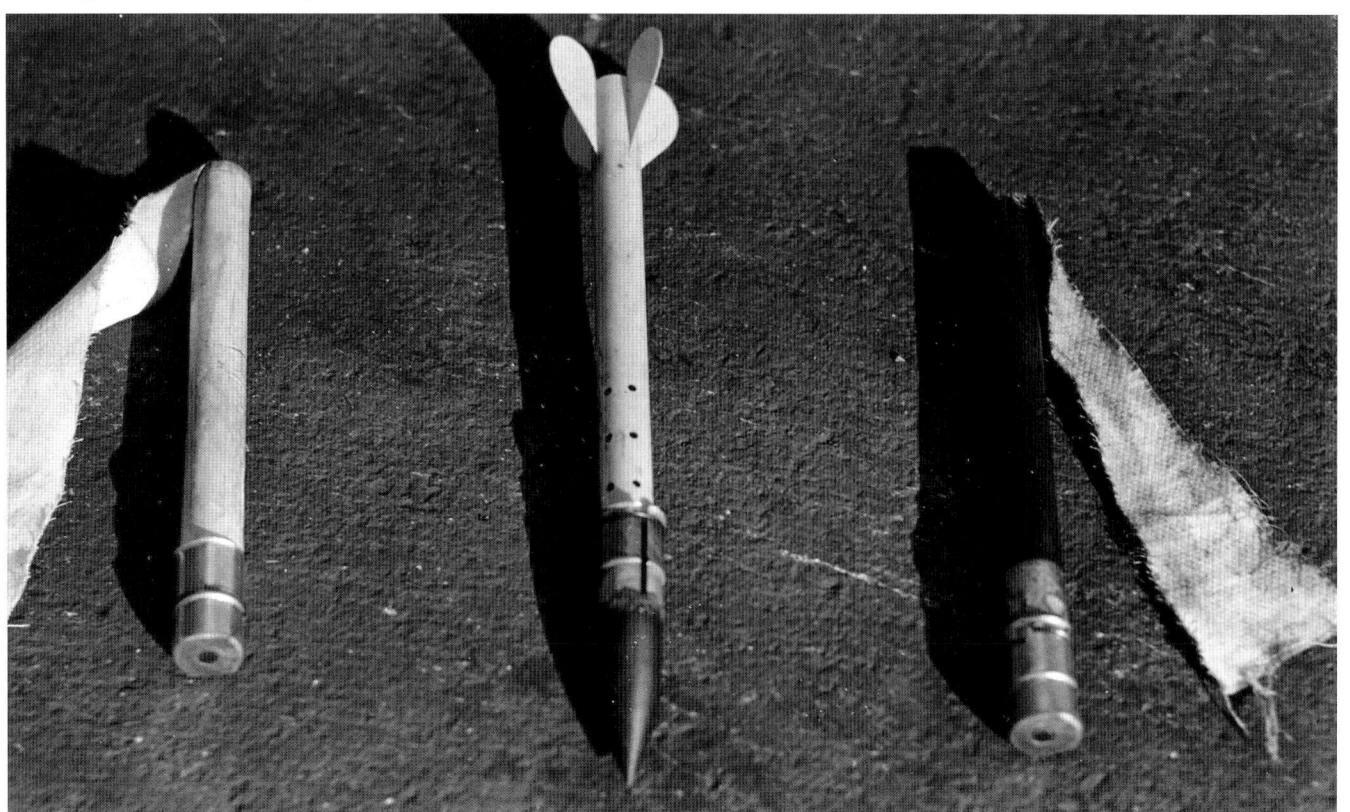

US air-dropped flares and an incendiary dart (center).

Interesting wartime cutaway showing German light bombs and their fuses. A 10 kg Carbonit bomb is in the center.

A German observer uses a 12.5 kg bomb to demonstrate the basics of his part-time job as a bombardier.

Night bomber: This LVG C.II carries a particularly heavy bomb load with six 50 kg PuW bombs beneath the wings and four 12.5 kg PuW bombs on fuselage racks.

A German 20kg (44 pound) Carbonit bomb, featuring a cast-iron body, and a ring-shaped stabilizing fin. These were normally filled with TNT.

A wartime French postcard showing a German 300 kg PuW bomb that failed to explode.

Posing with a 100 kg bomb recovered from a Gotha bomber crash near Ypres during September 1918.

The observer as bombardier: A posed shot to show how the observer would deliver a 10kg Carbonit bomb by hand. Note the observer's Parabellum MG 14.

British troops look over 4.5 and 20kg Carbonit bombs captured in the Mesopotamian campaign during 1918.

A French soldier reviews a German 300 kg PuW bomb.

Gotha ground crews handling 12.5 kg, 50 kg, and 100 kg bombs, along with a 300 kg PuW bomb carried on a simple cart.

A 300 kg PuW bomb assembled before loading on a Gotha GV.

The simple origins of ground attack: Loading M1917 Stielhandgranate into wooden racks for use by the observer aboard a Halberstadt CL.II. The fuse for the Stielhandgranate burned for approximately 4.5 seconds.

Loading "concentrated charges" aboard a Halberstadt CL.II. These were created by using six explosive charges from standard Stielhandgranate, wired around a central stick grenade as the detonator. Note the rack for five 2kg "Fliegermaus" fragmentation bombs, introduced in mid-1918.

Close combat from the air: Brunhilde's observer is armed with a plentiful supply of M1917 Stielhandgranate, along with flares and a Parabellum LMG 14 (equipped with a Oigee/Berlin .3 power telescopic sight).

Ready to attack England: A Gotha GV loaded with 50 and 100 kg bombs.

BOMBS & GRENADES

Ground crews load a Gotha GV. Two 100 kg PuW bombs are attached to the fuselage racks, while 50 kg bombs are added to the wing racks.

Fully loaded: A Gotha GV with 5x 50kg and 2x 100 kg PuW bombs.

Loading a 300 kg PuW bomb on the fuselage rack of a Gotha GV.

Loading 100 kg PuW bombs onto a Gotha GVb. Note the MG14 Parabellum MG in the front gunner's position.

CANNONS AND RECOILLESS GUNS

Flying artillery: France led the way in equipping aircraft with cannon. This Voisin IV displays its massive Hotchkiss Model 1885 37mm gun. The cannon was a single shot, hand-loaded weapon.

The Voisin IV pusher became the main flying gun platform for the Hotchkiss Model 1885 37mm gun. The pilot moved to the back seat and the gunner had a wide field of fire for his single shot cannon.

French Voisin IV with a Hotchkiss Model 1895 37mm gun. This cannon weighed nearly 325 pounds and fired a 1 ½ pound explosive shell.

The big 37mm Hotchkiss gun looks impressive, but documented successes with the cannon are rare. The recoil was overpowering, and the hand-loaded cannon filled the gunner's position with gun smoke when it fired.

The big gun nose: A Voisin X LBR fitted with a Hotchkiss 37mm Model 1902 cannon.

A Voisin X LBR fitted with a Hotchkiss 37mm Model 1902 cannon. Most of these aircraft were soon converted into the "LAR" bomber version.

The lance of the Norman Prince: A French Voisin mounting a long barrel 37mm Model 1895 gun.

A 37mm Hotchkiss "modele 1902" (short barrel). This cannon weighed 103 pounds and fired a 1-pound explosive shell.

The Davis Recoilless Gun mounted on the Naval Aircraft Factory N-1, a giant twin-engine floatplane. A M1918 Lewis Gun (made at Savage Arms) is mounted atop the Davis Gun to fire spotting rounds.

The Davis gun mounted in the nose of a Curtiss F-5-L flying boat, a nearly 14,000-pound aircraft. Note the "collecting bag" attached to the Lewis Gun to capture spent casings.

The Naval Aircraft Factory N-1 floatplane in testing: note the Davis Gun visible above the top wing.

The Curtiss F-5-L flying boat armed with the Davis Gun in the nose observer/gunner position.

The Davis Gun aboard a Curtiss F-5-L. Ultimately, the giant Curtiss flying boats were operated by US Naval Aviators flying from Naval Air Stations in England and France during 1918. Note the shoulder stock mounted on the side of the Davis Gun.

A cut-away of the Curtiss F-5-L on display at the Philadelphia Navy Yard.

The Short S.81 Gun-Carrier shown equipped with a Vickers 1 ½-pounder gun. The British later used this aircraft to test the American Davis recoilless gun.

The nose position of the Curtiss F-5-L flying boat. The rotating mount was originally designed for the F-5-L's forward defense Lewis MGs.

The Davis Gun weighed recoilless gun weighed nearly 210 pounds (for the 6-pounder version) with the weapon and mount. Note the details of the Davis and its attached M1918 Lewis gun.

On dry land: Full view of the Davis Gun and its attached Lewis MG, mounted on the nose of a Curtiss F-5-L flying boat.

The 37mm COW Aircraft Cannon: Made by Coventry Ordnance Works, the COW was a long-recoil operated weapon, firing either semi or full automatic (60 rpm). Two were mounted in DH4s for combat tests during late 1918, but the project did not go forward.

The "Canon de 37mm, modele 1918, Puteaux", a semi-automatic cannon mounted in a Hispano-Suiza engine. A 5-round magazine can be seen at the top of barrel. This gun was intended for SPAD fighters and a few may have seen combat trials in the last month of the war.

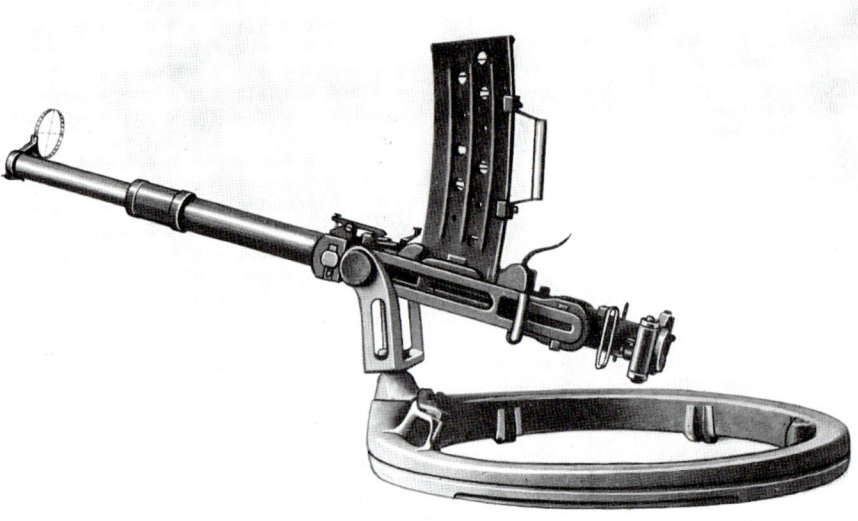

An isolation view of a ring-mounted Becker 20mm Type 2 aircraft cannon. Note the handle attached to the heavy (11-pound) magazine.

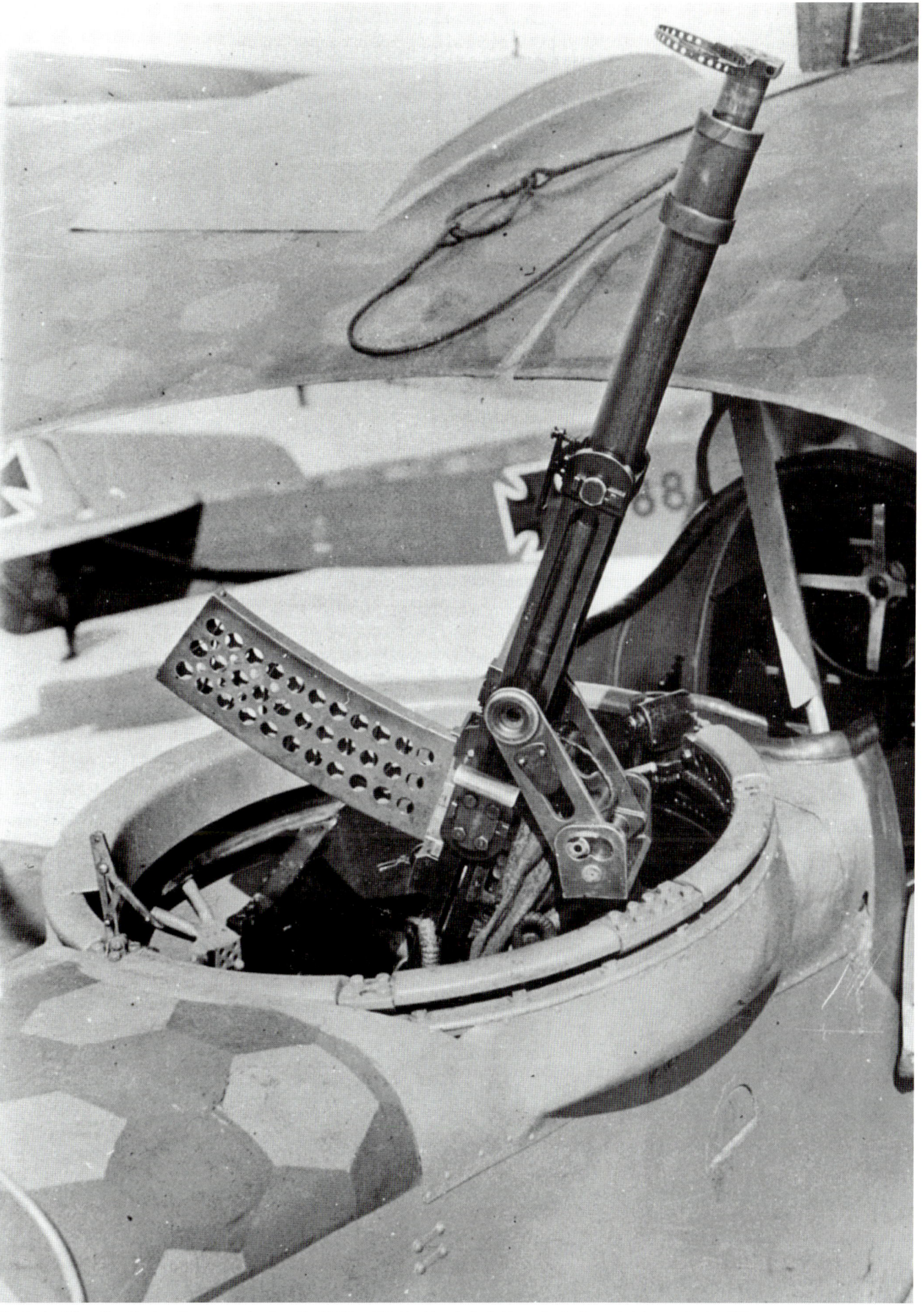
The Becker 20mm Type 2 automatic cannon, chambered in 20x70mmRB. Fired by a butterfly trigger, the Becker cycled at approximately 325 rpm.

Originally designed for ground attack work, the Becker 20mm auto cannon was also issued as an observer's gun and used in air-to-air combat. Note the details of the 12-round magazine.

A 20mm Becker cannon aboard a Hansa-Brandenburg W19 floatplane. Note the details of the thumb-activated butterfly trigger.

The Becker Type 2 20mm cannon would become the pattern for the Swiss Oerlikon 20mm gun, as well as the German MG FF aircraft cannon of WWII.

Detail view of the Becker 20mm Type 2 handgrip, trigger, and ring mount on the Hansa-Brandenburg W19 floatplane.

The beginnings of anti-tank aircraft: An armored Albatross J.1 equipped with a Becker 20mm cannon for ground attack, including tank attack. A Model 1913/17 MG can be seen on the opposite side of the observer's position.

Henri Farré (1871-1934)

Farré trained in Paris and then became a successful artist living abroad. When WWI began in 1914, he returned to France and joined the Service Aeronautique. Farre regularly flew as an observer, recording his combat views as sketches and then finished them as large oil paintings. Ultimately, Farre would be awarded the Legion of Honor and the Croix de Guerre for his work. Lieutenant Farre's incredible work was among the first to record the scope, the action, and the terrible realities of aerial combat. We present it here as a tribute to all the brave pilots and observers that served in World War One.

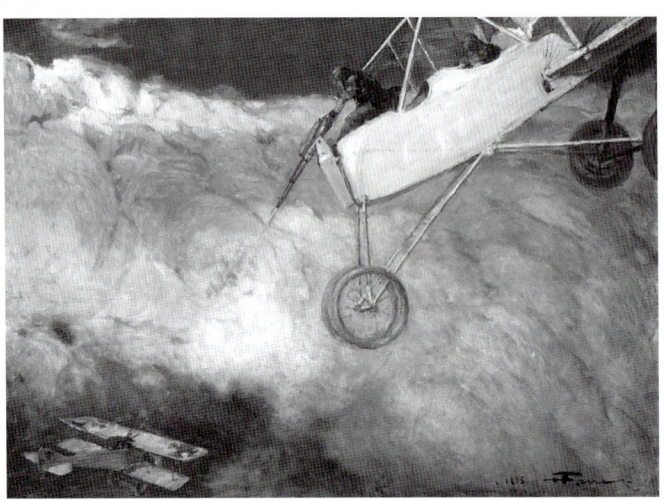